THE AMERICAN MIND MEETS THE MIND OF CHRIST

ROBERT KOLB, EDITOR

CONCORDIA
SEMINARY PRESS
light from above

The American Mind Meets the Mind of Christ

Concordia Seminary Press

ISBN 978-0-911770-75-9

801 Seminary Place, St. Louis, Missouri 63105

Contents

Preface

Robert Kolb

The American Mind Meets the Mind of Christ

One of the Latin words the ancient Romans used to designate a priest, "pontifex," means "bridge-builder." When the writer to the Hebrews spoke of Jesus Christ as the great high priest (especially chapters 7–9), he described the Lord's function as our mediator, the one who rebuilds the bridge between sinners and God. Jesus sent his disciples into the world, to the "nations" or cultures of the human race, to build the bridge between himself and those who have rebelled against him, between the life-restoring Word of God and those who prefer listening only to themselves or some other creature. God calls his baptized children to restore the connection between those who have strayed from him—who live in opposition to his way of life—and their Creator, who wishes to be their Father. Since individuals always live in the midst of communities, the address of the Gospel to individual sinners always meets them within the context of their communities, their cultures. This volume seeks to aid North American Christian bridge-builders at the beginning of the twenty-first century in carrying out the task of bringing God into conversation with those around us outside the faith.

God so shaped human creatures as individuals that they reflect something of his own rich complexity, his own intricate and multifaceted nature. He also created people for community: it was not good that Adam be alone (Gn 2:18). In human communities, the rich and intricate nature of human life comes to full bloom as individuals share their own gifts and talents and contribute them to the whole. God binds together the whole of the life of all individual human beings into specific groups we call "cultures." Sometimes these cultures are coterminous with linguistic or political groupings, and sometimes they are not.

Culture may be defined in many ways because the term embraces and mirrors the complexity and wonder of what God wrought in creating the human being. The term refers to the organic and dynamic whole of human activities and relationships which define the meaning and significance of life for a specific group of people. A culture is organic because it consists of mutually-related elements which are influencing and shaping each other, often even when they do not appear to be related to, or relevant for, each other. It is dynamic in that its elements are always in movement and development, experiencing and effecting change, even when they often appear to shift with only glacial speed. The various elements in culture are linked by a common identity and purpose in a host of common endeavors, and they presume a body of shared assumptions, values, and allegiances. The people of a culture are "of one mind," in the sense that even with all their individual differences and their unique ways of looking at the world, they share certain presuppositions about life and its meaning. They approach many aspects of life from much the same definition of life's goals and purposes, even when they cannot readily articulate that definition.

Parenthetically, we should note that the institutions within a culture have their own cultures. Or perhaps more precisely, they constitute subcultures. The church, too, has always existed as a distinct cultural unit within the peoples and lands, the societies and cultures, into which the Holy Spirit has placed it. In this volume, however, we are not looking at the culture of the church but rather the culture of the North American societies into which God calls his people to give witness to his Word. This is the place where he has called us to build bridges to those who do not know him as Lord and Savior.

North American culture is one of the many places into which God has called his people, and it is a different culture in 2010 than the American culture in which many living Christians have grown up. Events in recent months and years have, in different ways, radically changed the landscape of the continent. Economic recession has raised doubts and fears about personal future, though seemingly without raising considerable questions regarding the American dream, the American way of understanding life. The election of a president of the United States of African ancestry marks a symbolic step in the pursuit of traditional American values of offering all possibilities to all citizens, even though, it is to be feared, the actual situation of many disadvantaged African-Americans has not changed with the election of Barack Obama. In this decade the experience of the church of Jesus Christ has given the expression "going south" a new and positive meaning as the Global South becomes the Holy Spirit's stage for his demonstration of the power of his Word in the twenty-first century. But this is not in every respect the onset of a new golden age in the church. Among intellectuals the retreading of old arguments in the "New Atheism," as tired and worn-out as these arguments may seem to us, reminds us that the struggle against the father of lies (Jn 8:44) continues. On the popular level in North America, it takes other forms. Since about 1980, and particularly since 2000, increasing numbers of Christians have experienced encounters with levels of antagonism toward the Christian faith that had previously not existed in North America. They voice the claim that the context for witnessing to Christ on this continent seems more hostile, or at least more indifferent, as the public's biblical literacy declines and assertive presentations of alternate worldviews increase. Polls note a decline in public affirmation of traditional expressions of biblical ethics. Public spaces in American society—the workplace, the city hall, the big-box store—have become increasingly more complicated places for Christians to speak authentically and intelligibly of their faith.

Because the conversation between God and his human creatures is, by God's design, an exchange of ideas and messages, it is important for Christians to understand those with whom they speak. God's communication to those outside the faith does address these human beings as the creatures he fashioned them to be, with intelligible claims and comprehensible offers of God's goodness and mercy. God's Word, to be sure, is always higher than our thoughts, and always has an element of inscrutability about it (Rom 11:33–36). At the same time, God communicates his love in expressible and explicable fashion. God's way of thinking meets human ways of thinking within the framework of his created order for communication.[1]

Every culture in which God gives his gifts has developed its own forms for speaking of reality, for cultural evaluation of the world around and in the midst of its people. In 1987 Allan Bloom sparked widespread discussion of the changing tone and substance of American public culture with his book, *The Closing of the American Mind*. This book was one of a number in the period that examined the mentality or worldview of Americans. Since that time "the American mind" has been the subject of wide-ranging investigations and discussions as Americans have tried to explore and analyze the ideological currents that shape contemporary thought in our society.

The Bible also describes the fundamental orientation of human beings to the world around them with phrases that have been translated with the word "mind." "Mind" in this sense, it must be noted, is not a synonym for "reason" or rational thought processes. This "mind" embraces the fundamental attitudes formed as reason, will, and emotions combined to direct individuals and groups along the course they determine to follow. "Mind" is the disposition or inclination that guides and focuses thinking and action. "Have this mind among yourselves which you have in Christ Jesus," Paul admonished the Philippians (2:5). In 1 Corinthians 2:14, Paul reminded his readers that "we have the mind of Christ," Christ's way of thinking and, therefore, of acting. This way of thinking is not oriented toward what God has made but toward God himself, in contrast to our sinful way of thinking (Phil 3:19). The mind of Christ frames life within the structures God fashioned for human living. It is brought into sinners' way of thinking through baptismal death to sinful identity and resurrection as children of God (Col 3:2–4, read in the context of Col 2:11–15). When Christ healed or liberated the man possessed of a demon, that man was returned to "his right mind," that is, the kind of thinking that governs life in the way God made humanity to live in the first place (Lk 8:35). This godly "mind" or way of thinking designates the fundamental disposition a person has toward life, our foundational convictions about reality, our framing explanation for life.

At the heart of all the variety of human "minds" are views of whatever is Absolute or Ultimate in life. Many people designate the Absolute or Ultimate in their lives as "god." Our prosperity and other forms of good fortune permit us often not to worry about the Absolute and Ultimate, as people in most cultures through history have had to do. Therefore, it may be that those around us, and we ourselves, do not think within such grander horizons but rather seek on a practical, day-to-day basis just whatever has the power to "deliver the goods," "to make things work," "to keep me safe and my boat from going belly-up." Moreover, we often do not need to look to that which holds our lives together. Luther defined the term "god" in the Large Catechism (in his explanation of the First Commandment) as that which serves as the source of all good in our lives, and as our haven in time of distress. He also explained that whatever commands our (ultimate) trust is really serving as our god.[2] We search for reliable objects of that core, orienting trust in life because we need and seek from them a sense of identity, a sense of security, and a sense of meaning.

Americans look to a variety of objects to give them a sense of identity or security or meaning. The history of our nation and its people has led us to fashion a number of alternatives to the Christian "mind" and message or to invent supplements to the God who has come as Jesus of Nazareth. These false alternatives to the true God, the triune God, challenge the Christian faith and invite Christian witness in the twenty-first century.

Preparation for that witness includes assessing how those to whom we are called to bring his message of salvation think, how they assess the reality of their lives.

From the time of Luther on, Lutherans have always had a two-edged attitude toward the cultures into which God has placed them. H. Richard Niebuhr's analysis of the church and its relationships to culture, above all in his *Christ and Culture*, published in 1951, dubbed Luther's view "Christ and Culture in Paradox." His valuable analysis was not well served by this title since it misrepresents what Luther really thought about God's gift of culture, damaged as it always is by sin. Luther loved paradoxes, but it is no paradox to posit that human life takes place in two dimensions, "two kingdoms" or "realms," as this concept is often labeled, and that different things happen in each.[3] Luther came to this conclusion on the basis of an anthropology which distinguishes between being human in relationship to God as God's gift, and being human in relationship to God's other creatures as the human performance of God's expectations for human living. This way of analyzing what it means to be human the reformer called "the distinction between two kinds of righteousness."[4]

Against the background of this element of Luther's thought, Lutherans have both affirmed the created goodness of their cultures, and at the same time, served as sharp critics of what their cultures do in opposition to God's will. In the "heartlands" of Lutheranism in central and northern Europe, Lutherans generally have found themselves dominant in their cultures and often were subverted into being pillars of the culture more than critics. But a strong tradition of cultural criticism appeared in Nordic and German lands at decisive times. The persecuted Lutheran churches of the lands of the Counter-Reformation east of Germany and the Scandinavian kingdoms were often cut off from the cultural power centers. Nonetheless, they still played key roles in cultural development, of the language, literature, and historical writing of peoples such as the Slovaks, the Latvians, and the Estonians, when they emerged as nations around their own distinct cultures, in the nineteenth century. In the course of the early modern period, the immigrant churches that came into existence in Australia, South Africa, Latin and North America found themselves most often not dominant within the prevailing "English," "Spanish," or "Portuguese" cultures of their new lands. But they could often ally themselves with that dominant Christian culture and make themselves at least somewhat comfortable in their new environment. The Lutheran mission churches that have emerged in the wake of the Reformation, from the seventeenth century onward, as European and later other Lutherans sent out missionaries to bring new peoples to Christ, have often lived in conflict with traditional cultural values but have also attempted to affirm and enrich those values. One of the greatest challenges for contemporary North American Lutherans, as we confront more and more aspects in our own culture that seem in conflict with God's plan for human life, is to balance our proclamation of God's law as critical judgment and our affirmation of God's providential goodness in the facets of our culture that reflect his goodness.

The faculty colleagues of Concordia Seminary, Saint Louis, who have written the essays in this volume, have tried to illustrate both the affirmation of selected cultural characteristics and the cultural criticism that comes naturally to our lips. Each author has approached his topic in his own way. Not every essay in this volume presents an analysis of both sides of the phenomena under discussion. Not every essay offers direct assistance for engaging these cultural trends with the proclamation of law and gospel. But the collection of approaches presented here should aid readers in developing their own ability to sort out factors of culture that they and their people confront in daily life and treat them in a variety of ways as Lutheran Christians and theologians. In that way, it is hoped, this volume may contribute to sharpening the bridge-building skills of all its readers.

Each winter, for the past fourteen years, the annual College of Fellows of the Institute for Mission Studies of Concordia Seminary, Saint Louis, has gathered faculty members from the Seminary and staff members from the International Center of The Lutheran Church–Missouri Synod for discussions of critical issues in the mission from which God sends his church. The 2007 College of Fellows addressed aspects of the current "American mind" in order to discuss how Christian witness may best engage these alternatives to the gospel of Jesus Christ. Nine essays written by Concordia Seminary theologians were prepared to aid Seminary faculty and students to bring the biblical message to the North American context in which God has called us to proclaim his Word. These essays, revised and updated, are offered here to challenge the church to active discussion and practice of Christ's mission in the world. The thoughts of the essayists may serve readers as building materials for the construction of bridges into the lives of those whom they encounter and who engage them in conversation about Jesus Christ. Christian witness begins with a deconstruction of false views of reality, and it comes to completion by bringing the promise of new life in Christ to construct a biblical "mind" in the midst of the (post)modern world. This volume is designed to support effective witness to the faith in our individual contexts into which God places us.

The volume has been made possible by a generous gift from Peace Lutheran Church in Chicago. This congregation, founded in 1902, concluded its service to God and its community in 2005. In assigning its assets it graciously made funding available to the Institute for Mission

Studies for several projects. We are grateful to the members of Peace congregation, including Mr. and Mrs. Charles Bennett, and to the last of its seven pastors, Luther G. Albrecht, for enabling us to bring these essays to the church.

Endnotes

[1] This reflects Luther's understanding of what it means to be human and the way in which God's Word works within human life. See Robert Kolb and Charles P. Arand, *The Genius of Luther's Theology: A Wittenberg Way of Thinking for the Contemporary Church* (Grand Rapids: Baker, 2008).

[2] Large Catechism, Ten Commandments, First Commandment, 1–4: *The Book of Concord*, ed. Robert Kolb and Timothy J. Wengert (Minneapolis: Fortress, 2000), 386–387; *Die Bekenntnisschriften der evangelisch-lutherischen Kirche* (11. ed.; Göttingen: Vandenhoeck & Ruprecht, 1992), 560–561.

[3] Robert Kolb, "Niebuhr's 'Christ and Culture in Paradox' Revisited," *Lutheran Quarterly* 10 (1996): 259–279.

[4] See Kolb and Arand, *Genius of Luther's Theology*, 9–130.

Health and Wealth

Dale A. Meyer

Living in the Land of Milk and Honey

"The person who dies with the most toys wins."

"Thou shalt not covet."

Can you imagine your parishioners in the following scene? From the movie *Talladega Nights*, NASCAR driver Ricky Bobby (played by comedian Will Ferrell) offers grace in his huge new house.

> Dear Lord Baby Jesus ... We thank you so much for this bountiful harvest, Domino's and KFC and the always delicious Taco Bell. I just want to take time to say thank you for my family, my two beautiful, handsome, striking sons, Walker and Texas Ranger, or TR as we call him, and of course my red-hot smoking wife, Carley, who's a stone cold fox... Also want to thank you for my best friend and teammate, Cal Naughton, Jr. who's got my back no matter what...

Wife Carley interrupts to tell Ricky he should stop referring to "baby Jesus" because Jesus grew up. Everyone starts talking about what Jesus they like to pray to. That's too much for Carley who says, "I want you to do this grace good so that God will let us win tomorrow." She should have saved her breath. Ricky resumes his prayer:

> Dear 8-pound, 6-ounce newborn infant Jesus ... we just thank you for all the races I've won, and the $21.2 million ...Whew! Love that money that I have accrued over this past season

> also due to a binding endorsement contract that stipulates that I mention "PowerAde" at each grace. I just want to say that PowerAde is delicious and it cools you off on a hot summer day and we look forward to PowerAde's release of Mystic Mountain Blueberry. Thank you for all your power and your grace, dear Baby God. Amen.

Here's hoping you don't have congregational members who are blatant, me-centered religious people who have fashioned Jesus to their own specifications in a lusty pursuit of earthly goods that corrupts traditional Christianity. Long ago, doctors worked to defeat tuberculosis, commonly called "consumption," and ministers preached against "the almighty dollar" and materialism. In our more recent past, there have been new strains of the love of money that seemed resistant to traditional Sunday morning prescriptions. It's "consumerism"—a new "consumption"—that has had people seeking to acquire and buy at an ever more frantic pace. Restless to get the newest gadget, restless to check out the newest specialty store, restless to shop even on vacations in the most scenic places in the world, spending as the antidote for restlessness. The Ricky Bobby scene is effective satire because it still reflects the searching of so many people today. Both members and non-members of churches are demonstrating the first part of Augustine's famous line, "Our hearts are restless..." I do not think it would be too bold to say that this restless consumerism motivated in large part the behaviors that made the downturn in the world's economies in late 2008 and 2009 inevitable. Moreover, I suspect that neither this consumptive consumerism nor the restlessness it inevitably fosters has been altered much by the current "great recession." It may even be that the restlessness has spread and been intensified by the loss of investment income, homes, and jobs. But most citizens of the United States betray an underlying optimism. Like Ricky Bobby, we are down but never out. Most hope, even if against hope, that their lifestyles and levels of material prosperity will not be modified much over the long haul. Few have publicly declared any fundamental change in their belief that a large measure of contentment and security, even if not necessarily happiness, can be found in a checkbook or an investment account. In this sense, the fact that people are currently buying less and saving more is merely (and literally!) the flip side of the same consumerist coin.

The following article takes a look at material prosperity in the book of Deuteronomy and suggests some ways that pastoral preaching and teaching might, *might* make the good people of our congregations understand that today's rampant consumerism is, at the heart, a First Commandment issue. If our preaching and teaching can arouse people's attention, the Spirit might lead them to confess with their material "stuff" the truth of Augustine's whole line, "Our hearts are restless until they rest in Thee" (*Confessions* I.1).

"Man does not live by bread alone but by every word that proceeds from the mouth of the Lord (Dt 8:3; Lk 4:4)." That passage, quoted by Jesus against the devil, acknowledges that *we do need material things* to live, and therefore we devote time and energy to acquiring things. In our particular economic system, that works itself out as businesses entice consumers to buy whatever product they are offering. The acquisition may be a necessity, like food or clothing that is prepared and packaged simply enough to meet the need, or the product may be jazzed up to give us what we need and then some. For many Americans, contentment with the basic necessities is not enough (cf. 1 Tim 6:6–10). So our consumerist economy also pitches luxuries that aren't needed. "Sky Mall," the catalog that airlines put in seat pockets, advertised a self-propelled pool float in its Summer 2007 edition. Sitting on this float, you can move around your swimming pool with no physical effort, a wonderful thing because it frees you to manage the drink that the fancy float lets you take with you. Go ahead and rail against the excesses of the system, but this is the way our economy works and it's not likely to change. As flawed and self-indulgent as it often is, the capitalistic system is one humanly devised expression of a basic truth about our status as creatures of the unseen Creator. **As creatures we are bound to space and we are bound to time.** How we creatures bound by space and time should use the things of space and time, "stuff" in popular jargon, is a theme of Deuteronomy; how God, jealous for his people's devotion, wants them to live in his land of milk and honey.

What Israelite thought about how to handle abundance when they had no straw to make bricks? How often did an Israelite associate God with abundance when they had no alternative but to scrounge around in the wilderness? God promised the wandering Israelites that their new home would be a land of milk and honey; that they were on the verge of entering a place amazingly different from anything they had ever known. These promises of abundance no doubt helped draw the people onward through the hardships of the wilderness.

> He will love you and bless you and increase your numbers. He will bless the fruit of your womb, the crops of your land—your grain, new wine and olive oil—the calves of your herds and the lambs of your flocks in the land that he swore to your ancestors to give you. You will be blessed more than any other people... (Dt 7:13–14).

> For the Lord your God is bringing you into a good land—a land with streams and pools of water, with springs flowing in the valleys and hills; a land with wheat and barley, vines and fig trees, pomegranates, olive oil and honey; a land where bread will not be scarce and you will lack nothing; a land

> where the rocks are iron and you can dig copper out of the hills (Dt 8:7–9).

And there can be second helpings with no guilt!

> When the Lord your God has enlarged your territory as he promised you, and you crave meat and say, 'I would like some meat,' then you may eat as much of it as you want (Dt 12:20).

Stuff is OK. It's so OK that God has given material possessions the protection of a commandment, "Thou shalt not steal" (Ex 20:15). This command is more than "Don't take what doesn't belong to you." This prohibition is set in the context of God wanting us to value the material possessions that he graciously has given to us and to others. Even the order of the commandments shows the value of possessions. After God tells us in the first commandments how he wants us to worship and serve him (in our being, in our words and in our management of time), the unseen God directs us how to interact with others, with people we can see. We are to honor his representatives to us (parents and others in authority). Then we safeguard the lives of others ("Thou shalt not kill"), honor marriage ("Thou shalt not commit adultery"), and what's next? After life and marriage come possessions. "Thou shalt not steal." Following that comes the command that protects something as important as the neighbor's life, spouse, and possessions—the neighbor's reputation ("Thou shalt not bear false witness against thy neighbor").

How do those ancient promises of God-given material prosperity relate to America? America is not the new Promised Land, though early American religionists portrayed it that way, a new iteration of the ancient land of God's special presence. America is indeed a blessed land, blessed by God. "He causes his sun to rise on the evil and the good, and sends rain on the righteous and the unrighteous" (Mt 5:45). Living in America's abundance are some of God's new people in Christ. "The New Testament is concealed in the Old; the Old Testament is revealed in the New." Through the lens of the New Testament, we can apply Deuteronomy's passages about prosperity to our vocation as God's people living in American materialism and consumerism. The abundance promised to ancient Israel in Deuteronomy suggests that we need not be embarrassed by the material and financial wealth that many Americans and American church-goers have amassed. To be embarrassed that you have a luxury car or a big screen TV or even a self-propelled pool float can veer toward the extreme of asceticism. On the other hand, not having a second thought about the luxuries you're able to acquire falls into the other extreme of blind materialistic consumerism, like the Bobby family. Deuteronomy taught a middle way of both the material and the non-material to appreciate God's lordship. "He humbled you, causing you to hunger and then feeding you with manna, which neither you nor your ancestors had known, to teach you that people do not live on bread alone but on every word that comes from the mouth of the Lord" (Dt 8:3). The New Testament does the same. "Seek first his kingdom and his righteousness, and all these things will be given to you as well" (Mt 6:33).

That we are bound to space and time but our Creator is not so bound means we live in a tension between the material nature of life and the unseen nature of God. God's bounty can result in temptation to idolatry. Because the nations around Israel had religions rooted in the seen world of nature, Deuteronomy stressed that the unseen nature of God should dominate life in the land of milk and honey. Their abundance was a mediated encounter with God, not an immediate contact as the heathen nations imagined with their various nature religions. **Although God had given ancient Israel their abundance, he had not revealed himself to Israel in a physical form and he wanted their devotion to him kept that way.**

> You shall not make for yourself an image in the form of anything in heaven above or on the earth beneath or in the waters below (Ex 20:4; Dt 5:8).
>
> Cursed is anyone who makes an idol—a thing detestable to the Lord, the work of skilled hands—and sets it up in secret (Dt 27:15).
>
> You yourselves know how we lived in Egypt and how we passed through the countries on the way here. You saw among them their detestable images and idols of wood and stone, of silver and gold. Make sure there is no man or woman, clan or tribe among you today whose heart turns away from the Lord our God to go and worship the gods of those nations (Dt 29:16–18).

No small part of the temptation to idols was that their value could be seen, a contrast to the unseen God.

> Do not covet the silver and gold on them [idols] (Dt 7:25).

The modern American materialist addicted to consumerism is ultimately motivated by the same impulse that tempted the peoples around Israel. That's the innate Law. "When the Gentiles, who do not have the Law, do by nature things required by the Law, they are a law for themselves, even though they do not have the Law, since they show that the requirements of the Law are written on their hearts" (Rom 2:14–15). At creation, Adam and Eve had a perfect knowledge of God and a sinless and totally satisfying communion with him. Sin, however, destroyed that perfect relationship, obscured the inborn Law, and so made us descendants of Adam and Eve dependent upon the message of Holy Scripture for a clearer and saving knowledge of God. That corrective divinely provided, the inborn Law still remains in every heart, fuzzy though it be and usually not acknowledged as from God. Every person has that inborn yearning for communion with God, but apart from Scripture God gets remade, fashioned according to the sinner's imagination. Xenophanes, a fifth century B.C. critic of religion, said, "If the ox could paint a picture, his god would look like an ox." And that's what the peoples around Israel did, fashioned gods after their own imaginings ("gross idolatry"). These man-made idols were attempts to satisfy their yearning for the satisfying communion with God that is driven by the inborn Law (cf. Eccl 3:11). This idolatry was even more seductive because the idols were the works of men's hands, as opposed to unmerited grace (cf. Eph 2:8-9) and because these idols could be seen, as opposed to the difficult proposition of living by faith and not sight (2 Cor 5:7). The rampant consumerism that is ravaging America meets these three criteria. It is a material manifestation of trying to satisfy our innate desire for satisfaction by desiring created things rather than the Creator (cf. Rom 1:25). Consumerism fits in nicely with the deep-seated sin of works righteousness. And you can see consumerism work; you can own it, possess it, and be devoted to something seen rather than something unseen. And so the innate in-working Law has advanced long-standing American materialism to out-and-out consumerism, and vanity.

> Amidst our plenty something still...
> To me, to thee, to him is wanting!
> That cruel something unpossessed
> Corrodes and leavens all the rest.
> (Charles Wesley, "Upon Our Lord's Sermon on the Mount,"
> Discourse VIII, 20)

What do they say? Insanity is doing the same thing over and over but expecting different results. God warned ancient Israel about "gross" idolatry to man-made images, and God's people today need to be warned about the subtle, "fine" idolatry of materialism as consumerism.

So our message to God's people today is, "Beware the extremes and go down the middle." Our parishioners should be taught to know and feel that same tension between the seen and the unseen that God taught his ancient people in Deuteronomy. The God revealed in Jesus Christ still remains unseen. He has shown his "face" to us in his Son. "God, who said, 'Let light shine out of darkness,' made his light shine in our hearts to give us the light of the knowledge of the glory of God in the face of Christ" (2 Cor 4:6; see also Jn 1:18). This does not mean that we twenty-first century Christians have seen Jesus. We have not. "Though you have not seen him (Christ), you love him; and even though you do not see him now, you believe in him" (1 Pt 1:8). As "a holy nation, God's special possession" (1 Pt 2:9; cf. Dt 7:6), Christ-followers can use material things to our satisfaction but should do so aware of the tension between the seen and unseen (2 Cor 4:18; 5:7). "Is not life more important than food and the body more important than clothes? ...the pagans [Americans?] run after all these things, and your heavenly Father knows that you need them. But seek first his kingdom and his righteousness, and all these things will be given to you as well" (Mt 6:25, 32–33).

How can we under-shepherds help keep that tension taut? Words. Both in Deuteronomy and in our own American setting **that tension is to be kept taut by words, God's words coming to us to establish his reign in our hearts, physical words to hear, to read, to learn, remember and follow and share with one another, especially with our children.** Words are the physical "place," where the unseen makes itself most knowable and enters our creaturely world. While the Law drives us to futility, it does so in order that we will hear the physical word of the Gospel (Gal 3:22–24). That Gospel word makes the Means of Grace means of *grace*. Of Baptism the *Small Catechism* says, "The word of God in and with the water does these things." Of the Lord's Supper: "Given and shed for you for the forgiveness of sins." *These words, along with the bodily eating and drinking, are the main thing in the Sacrament.*

> [At Sinai] the Lord spoke to you out of the fire. You heard the sound of words but saw no form; there was only a voice. He declared to you his covenant, the ten commandments..." (Dt 4:12-13).

It was the kindness of God that he did not show any form of himself. "You cannot see my face, for no one may see me and live" (Ex 33:20). The cloud that veiled his presence on Sinai was his way of drawing near to his people without slaying them. His closeness, his nature as Immanuel, was known by the voice. *There was only a voice.*

> Hear, Israel, the decrees and laws I declare in your hearing today. Learn them and be sure to follow them. The Lord our God made a covenant with us at Horeb... The Lord spoke to you face to face out of the fire on the mountain (Dt 5:1, 4).

The words for living in the land of milk and honey are historic words, words from the exodus and the revelation at Sinai. There are not new revelations for each generation but words repeated from generation to generation.

> One generation will commend your works to another; they will tell of your mighty acts (Ps 145:4).

> The secret things belong to the Lord our God; but the things revealed belong to us and to our children forever, that we may follow all the words of this law (Dt 29:29).

The things revealed do include physical sights to Israel, but those are always distinct from any physical representation of God, the materialistic way that surrounding nations went about satisfying their need for communion with the Eternal. These *things revealed* were the saving events by which God had demonstrated his lordship with Israel, acts conveyed by words for the ongoing life of Israel, rather than ever new events to be appropriated by sight. It's obvious when you think about it; God's saving events were quite rare in the long course of Israel's history and had not been experienced by most individual members of the nation. Hence, those rare visible demonstrations of God's saving presence were remembered in the context of covenantal words, words of remembrance for those who had had some first-hand experience with the exodus and wilderness events, but for most Israelites the words were words of teaching to younger generations who hadn't been there.

> Watch yourselves closely so that you do not forget the things your eyes have seen or let them slip from your heart as long as you live. Teach them to your children and to their children after them. Remember the day you stood before the Lord your God at Horeb... (Dt 4:9-10).

> When your children ask you, "What is the meaning of the stipulations, decrees and laws the Lord our God has commanded you?" tell them: "We were slaves of Pharaoh in Egypt, but the Lord brought us out of Egypt with a mighty hand. Before our eyes the Lord sent signs and wonders... If we are careful to obey all this law before the Lord our God, as he has commanded us, that will be our righteousness" (Dt 6:20-22, 25).

As with the earlier application to Israel's plenty, so **the focus upon words transfers easily to the contemporary situation for us Christians living in this American land of milk and honey.** The tension between the seen and the unseen is to be kept taut by words, physical words heard, physical words read, physical words with water, bread and wine to bestow Gospel. So church leaders, pastors, teachers, and parents should give the highest importance to teaching the distinction between our culture's materialistic and consumerist life of sight, and the once, long ago seen revelation of God in foreshadowing saving acts of the Old Testament, the physical coming of his Son into the world, his active obedience, his leading us into freedom as our Passover, and the promise of a heavenly promised land. All that is present...now! We are not called to be the curators of a museum. All that is present now in the living and active word of the scriptural revelation by which the Spirit of God works faith in the Incarnate One. "You know that it was not with perishable things such as silver or gold that you were redeemed ... For you have been born again, not of perishable seed, but of imperishable, through the living and enduring word of God. This is the word that was preached ("Gospeled") to you" (1 Pt 1:18, 23, 25).

"Saint and sinner" means we are constantly in need of God's Spirit through the word to keep us in proper tension between the seen and the unseen. "It is God who works in you to will and to act in order to fulfill his good purpose" (Phil 2:13). What then are some ways we as pastors can use words to help keep our people properly focused on a God-pleasing balance between the material and non-material aspects of his total care for us?

One is to **keep telling our historical story as God's people**; just as the Israelite elders were told to tell the story to the next generation. The purpose is not to entertain with our stories but to use story to open the contemporary hearer's mind and heart for the Spirit's work. The story we tell is how God has dealt with his people through the ages—Bible history—but let's not forget that our listeners can also apply biblical teachings to the stories that are closer to their own time and experience. Stories of the Great Depression still resonate with many Americans and offer entries for teaching the balance between the seen and unseen.

> When the Lord your God brings you into the land he swore to your fathers, to Abraham, Isaac and Jacob, to give you—a land with large, flourishing cities you did not build, houses filled with all kinds of good things you did not provide, wells you did not dig, and vineyards and olive groves you did not plant—then when you eat and are satisfied, be careful that you do not forget the Lord, who brought you out of Egypt, out of the land of slavery (Dt 6:10–12).

Another way to keep the extremes of the seen material and the unseen things of grace and faith in balance is **common sense**. Take time in sermons and Bible classes to examine popular assumptions and the "conventional wisdom." "It's good that you work hard, but do you think all you have is finally earned and not given to you?"

> When you have eaten and are satisfied, praise the Lord your God for the good land he has given you. Be careful that you do not forget the Lord your God, failing to observe his commands, his laws and his decrees... Otherwise, when you eat and are satisfied, when you build fine houses and settle down, and when your herds and flocks grow large and your

> silver and gold increase and all you have is multiplied, then your heart will become proud and you will forget the Lord your God... You may say to yourself, "My power and the strength of my hands have produced this wealth for me." But remember the Lord your God, for it is he who gives you the ability to produce wealth, and so confirms his covenant... (Dt 8:10–14, 17–18).

One way to use common sense is **satire**. The Roman poet Horace defined satire as speaking the truth with a smile ("ridentem dicere vero," *Satire* I.1.24). Instead of trying to crush your hearers with 2x4 bludgeoning about how sinful they are, why not lead them to repentance by showing the nonsense of so much materialism and consumerism (cf. Rom 2:4)? We can argue that the Spirit works better when people's defenses are down, and satire can make that happen. Charles Dickens's "Scrooge" is always in season. Ricky Bobby's prayer is one example of effective satire that the popular media provides in abundance. You can adapt secular satire for the purpose of preaching divine truth.

Words teaching biblical **time-management** can also keep the material and non-material aspects of life in healthy balance. There are many books in Christian bookstores presenting time management but most are secular teachings with only a veneer of biblical jargon. Deeper biblical teaching is profoundly better because it summons us not to be more efficient but to give up obsession with efficiency for the sake of communing with the divine word. We take considerable time to get and maintain the material necessities and wants of life (cf. Gn 1:26). Offsetting those times of work with times of rest, times when even necessary work is left undone, puts regular reminders into our schedules that all is finally a matter of grace, the grace that saves us and the second meaning of grace, the ability God gives us to pursue good works (Ps 92; Is 30:15; Mt 11:28). Regularly scheduled times with grace include gathering for corporate worship and daily time for personal devotion. Time away from work was a duty in Deuteronomy.

> Observe the Sabbath day by keeping it holy, as the Lord your God commanded you. Six days you shall labor and do all your work, but the seventh day is a Sabbath to the Lord your God. On it you shall not do any work... (Dt 5:12–14).

You know a literal day of rest is no longer laid on us (Col 2:16–17), but rest with God is desperately needed. Retreat from work, even church work, to God's grace in Christ is even more needed in our 24/7/365 society by people...and by pastors! (cf. Mk 6:31).

Where that balance between work and rest is taught, other ways to balance the seen and unseen will have time to be more appreciated.

Quiet, unhurried reflection always leads the faithful to think about how we are living under his saving lordship. One of those ways is **proportionate giving**.

> Be sure to set aside a tenth of all that your fields produce each year...that you may learn to revere the Lord your God always (Dt 14:22, 23).

Our New Testament understanding is that giving should not be legalistic but a proportionate giving motivated by the Gospel (2 Cor 9:6–15). That helps keep the proper balance in the heart of the giver. While we give back to the Lord for many of his works in the world, in Deuteronomy and in Paul's collection for the saints, there is an eye toward those who do not share in our current abundance, **gifts and works of mercy**. In western culture "mercy" is a feeling we have toward someone worse off than we are, but in biblical thought "mercy" or "mercies" are those acts of loving-kindness that happen between people in relationship. God has brought us into relationship through Baptism and shows us "mercies" every day. Our common humanity with all people and communion with members of the church are relationships in which we should do "mercies," selfless acts of loving-kindness to others (cf. Jas 2:15–17). That was a strong emphasis in Deuteronomy.

> There need be no poor people among you... If anyone is poor among your people in any of the towns of the land that the Lord your God is giving you, do not be hardhearted or tightfisted toward them. Rather, be openhanded and freely lend them whatever they need (Dt 15:4, 7–8).

> At the end of every seven years you must cancel debts (Dt 15:1).

> If any of your people, men or women, sell themselves to you and serve you six years, in the seventh year you must let them go free. And when you release them, do not send them away empty-handed. Supply them liberally from your flock, your threshing floor, and your winepress. Give to them as the Lord your God has blessed you (Dt 15:12–14).

Finally, something we do not naturally desire but something our caring Father has shown time and time again that he will use with us is **discipline** (cf. Prv 3:11–12). Should words not get to our hearts, God promises judgment, a return to conditions like the forgotten slavery and wilderness wanderings.

> Because you did not serve the Lord your God joyfully and gladly in the time of prosperity, therefore in hunger and

thirst, in nakedness and dire poverty, you will serve the enemies the Lord sends against you (Dt 28:47–48).

To wrap it up, living in the balance between seen and unseen should come from hearts in which Gospel words are motivating expressions of the freedom God's Spirit gives (cf. Mk 7:21–22). Freedom is part and parcel of understanding the Ten Commandments. "I am the Lord your God who brought you out of Egypt, out of the land of slavery. You shall have no other gods before me" (Dt 5:6-7). After the First Commandment come the commandments that show us how God wants us to exercise our new freedom in space and time before him and with people. Lastly come, by Lutheran enumeration, the Ninth and the Tenth Commandments, commandments that get little press but that are ringing reaffirmations of the freedom God spoke in the prologue. "Thou shalt not covet" (Ex 20:17; Dt 5:21). These commandments are more than prohibitions against desiring what belongs to your neighbor. They are repeated and echoing affirmations of freedom. "Do not, my people, do not be drawn back into any form of bound slavery!" The slavery to which God's holy people could revert is not a slavery back in Egypt but a slavery of desire for another person more than a desire for our God and Deliverer or consuming desire for something more than for the Giver of all things (cf. Lk 14:26; Mt 19:16–22). "It is for freedom that Christ has set us free. Stand firm, then, and do not let yourselves be burdened again by a yoke of slavery" (Gal 5:1). **From first to last, living in the American land of milk and honey should for us be about the First Commandment.** "The person who dies with the most toys wins..." but still dies. "Love the Lord your God with all your heart and with all your soul and with all your strength" (Dt 6:5). Christian consumer, *Thou shalt not covet!*

A Sermon Outline on God's Total Care for Us

God's Two Helpings
Deuteronomy 8:3

The idea behind this sermon: the popular word "spiritual" has led many Americans either to divorce faith from material things or to hopelessly confuse them. Some parishioners probably don't connect Sunday morning words to all the "stuff" in their lives; others may interpret growing material abundance as proof of their worthiness before God. After this sermon, your listeners will understand that possessions are to be highly valued because they are part of God's total provision for his sinful children. If your listeners really "get it," they will become more avid consumers of God's word than of material blessings.

I. Introduction: **Many Americans are blessed to take a second helping.**
   A. It's not unusual to sit at the kitchen table and ask

for seconds. By the way, does your family sit together at the kitchen table?

B. Anyway, second helpings aren't always available (some Americans today, for many during the Great Depression, and in underdeveloped countries throughout the world).

C. The children of Israel:
    1. Little to eat during their slavery in Egypt and wilderness wanderings.
    2. In Deuteronomy God promised to bring them into a "land of milk and honey."

D. Our second helpings remind us that America, in its own way, is also a "land of milk and honey."

II. **How do you and I feel about the second helping, about our abundance of food and material "stuff"?**

A. Yes, I have thought about it. I am blessed but...
    1. Pastor, I have earned those second helpings and worked hard for my material prosperity. "God helps those who help themselves."
    2. Pastor answers: Good that you work and good that you know that God has blessed you, but consider Deuteronomy 8:3.
    3. Maybe you need to think more deeply about your material abundance.

B. When I consider those less well-off, I feel guilty about my second helpings, our good food thrown out, and so much of our material abundance.
    1. This is the opposite reaction. Instead of "I am entitled to what I have got," we feel shame because we have an abundance of material things.
    2. But consider this surprising passage: Deuteronomy 12:20.
    3. Maybe the correct view is someplace between guilt and entitlement.

C. Then again, maybe you have not thought about it.
    1. Consuming material things is just what you do.
    2. Let me ask: if Jesus Christ (who, by the way, had "no place to lay his head") is really Lord of your life, isn't the role of material "stuff" in your life something to think about?

D. Those are possible reactions to abundant second helpings of all kinds of material "stuff." Let's look more closely at our sermon text, Deuteronomy 8:3. How did God want his ancient people to live in a "land of milk and honey"? **How should followers of Jesus Christ live in our "land of milk and honey"?**

III. **God puts two "helpings" before us.**
   A. Let's shift our understanding of "helpings."
      1. The two "helpings" are not two plates of meat and potatoes, or of more and more material possessions, whatever it is you might crave.
      2. The two "helpings" are the material needs God gives us, like food, and the word God gives us.
   B. Deuteronomy 8:3
      1. *People do not live on bread alone but on every word that comes from the mouth of the Lord.*
      2. This is not an insignificant passage. Jesus quoted it in Luke 4:4 when the devil tempted him with all the material wealth of the world.
   C. God gives us two "helpings."
      1. Food and material possessions for our physical needs and wants.
      2. His word for our sinful souls.
   D. A table prayer used in Germany sums it up nicely.
      1. "Lord, two things are needed, daily bread and forgiveness of our sins. We pray that you give us both according to your grace. Amen."
      2. By the way, I asked this question before: Does your family sit together to eat? Anyway...

IV. "Two things are needed." Let's talk about **that second helping, God's Word.**
   A. As God used scarcity to humble the Israelites in the wilderness, God humbles us.
      1. He allows, sometimes sends, the setbacks of life to humble us.
      2. Aging humbles us.
      3. Most important, God's Law invites us to humility by showing us our many sins and our need for a Savior.
   B. When God brought ancient Israel out of slavery and into a promised land, he pointed ahead to the freedom he has given us in Jesus.
      1. Freedom in Jesus who overcame slavery to sin and the devil's power (Lk 4:1–13).
      2. A promised land in heaven (1 Pt 1:3–5).
   C. The truest and most satisfying abundance comes from the second "helping" God gives us: "Where there is forgiveness of sin, there is also life and salvation" (Luther, *Small Catechism*).

V. Conclusion: "**Please pass a second helping.**"
   A. Physical aging:
      1. When we were young, we sat around the table and wolfed down second and even third helpings.
      2. As we get older, we find that we eat less, that second helpings become less automatic.
   B. Spiritual maturation: following Jesus Christ means asking for more and more helpings of God's word because the older we get, the hungrier we get for forgiveness, life, and salvation.
   C. I asked earlier if you sit together to eat. Eating together is a practical way for families to share second helpings of God's food for both body and soul. Amen.

A Sermon Outline on the Tension between the Seen and the Unseen

"Nothing Happened but Words"
1 Kings 17:7–16

The idea behind this sermon: rather than seek security in material abundance, your listeners will want to spend more time with God in word and prayer because they are reminded that only he can give satisfying and lasting security. This sense of security comes from the promises of the Gospel which alone satisfies our desire for perfect communion with God.

I. Introduction: **Do we look for security in things seen or unseen?** That's a general challenge of the Christian life.
   A. We worship an unseen God and Savior (Jn 20:29; 1 Pt 1:8).
   B. Yet we are constantly busy with things we see.
II. A practical example of finding security.
   A. It's hard to trust God's promises to take care of us when our attention is dominated by our possessions and finances, by having them or lacking them.
   B. It's easiest to trust security we can own or hope to own (our homes, our possessions, our bank accounts).
      1. But that can become idolatrous ("fine idolatry").
      2. "You cannot serve both God and money" (Mt 6:24).
      3. We need the Spirit's help to "Seek first his kingdom and his righteousness, and [then to trust] all these things will be given to you as well" (Mt 6:33).

III. **God led the widow at Zarephath to learn her dependable security was in God's word of promise.**
   A. Her own resources were zilch.
      1. Severe drought and famine had reduced her to the despair of one last meal.
      2. Verses 7–12.
   B. Elijah challenged her to find her security in a promise from God, verses 13–14.
   C. The Spirit worked in her heart through that word of promise, verses 15–16.
      1. The widow obeyed.
      2. God kept his promise to her.

IV. **Words are the way God makes things happen.**
   A. After the stock market crash in October, 1929, President Hoover told Congress, "Words are not of any great importance in times of economic disturbance. It is action that counts." A year later Hoover's political opponent Franklin D. Roosevelt said, **"Nothing happened but words."** (Amity Shlaes, *The Forgotten Man*, pp. 92, 102).
   B. God's words of promise fulfilled in Christ bring us the greatest security, eternal salvation (2 Cor 1:20).
   C. God's words of promise also give us a present sense of security that possessions cannot give.
      1. God knows your situation (Mt 6:23).
      2. God meets our worried words with his promises to take care of us.
         a. For example, "Our Father who art in heaven..." (unseen God).
         b. "Give us this day our daily bread" (seen physical needs).
      3. God promises to take care of you as he sees best. He gives examples of how he has cared for others (the widow; Rom 15:4).
   D. And should we be tempted to feel secure because of our prosperity, God's words warn us: "You fool!" (Lk 12:20).

V. Conclusion: **"Nothing happened but words?"**
   A. Quite a lot happens when you are led to take God's word to heart!
   B. "Whom have I in heaven but you? And earth has nothing I desire besides you...my portion forever!" (Ps 73:25–26).

R. Reed Lessing

The Good Life: Health, Fitness, and Bodily Welfare

Introduction

It was thirty-two years ago and I was a junior in high school, doing what just about every junior in high school across America looks forward to—driving! For some reason "teaching Reed to drive" fell into the hands of my mother. There we were one day, in downtown Denver; me with my driver's permit, my mother with her seatbelt buckled and her life insurance paid up. Then it happened. As I went to change lanes, I came within inches of another car. My mother, in her own words, "had the big one." And from that point on her litany to me was, "Reed Lessing, remember that you always have a blind spot."

You know what she meant. There are areas on either side of a vehicle that cannot be seen in the rear view or side view mirrors. Many accidents happen because drivers fail to allow for the blind spot.

In broader usage, blind spots are any issues in life that are easily overlooked. In this paper I will address a glaring blind spot in the piety of most Christians—their bodies. Oh, don't get me wrong. Most Christians are outraged by certain sins against the body: homosexuality, lesbianism, prostitution, abortion, pornography, and physical violence, just to name a few. But what we are blind to is a far more common sin against the body. Far too many of the baptized abuse their bodies through lack of a proper diet and by ignoring the need for a regular exercise regimen. It is painfully true. One of our greatest blind spots is health, fitness, and bodily welfare.

To a large extent Christians neglect their bodies because the church has neglected the biblical doctrine of creation. Recovering this doctrine is the major aspect of this paper. But before we look specifically at it, as well as how the American mind regards health, fitness, and bodily welfare, it will be helpful to place this discussion about our bodies into its proper context.

Picture a wheel. It has a center and protruding from it are five spokes. In the center of the wheel is Christ's baptismal gift. New life in Christ is both the glue that holds the five spokes together as well as the power that enables them to function properly. Moving out from this core of the wheel's center are the five "spokes" of wellness; they are (1) emotions, (2) relationships with people, (3) intellect, (4) vocation, and (5) health, fitness, and care of the body. To be whole means to keep these spokes connected to the wheel which informs and empowers their proper use. God has created everything to have balance: from the solar system, to the ecosystem, to our lives. If one spoke is neglected, the wheel will be out of balance.

That being said, addressing one aspect of the wheel is overly simplistic and even dangerous. God has made us in such a way that these components are interrelated. This study recognizes these dangers, even as it progresses in its discussion of physical health and wellness.

To begin, the status of America's physical health is reaching an all-time low. Obesity is the second leading cause of preventable death in the United States.[1] Approximately 127 million adults are overweight, 60 million obese, and 9 million severely obese. The number of adults who are overweight or obese continues to increase.[2] Currently 64.5% of U.S. adults, age 20 years and older, are overweight while 30.5% are obese. Qoheleth provides a fitting, if not sarcastic, commentary on these numbers: "All man's efforts are for his mouth, yet his appetite is never satisfied" (Eccl 6:7).

The American Mind: Reject the Body

The first attitude toward issues concerning the body is to reject it. Gnosticism, in many shapes and forms, continues to impact American society. Perhaps 1 Timothy 6:20 is the earliest Christian reaction to this movement. Paul instructs Timothy, "Timothy, guard what has been entrusted to your care. Turn away from godless chatter and the opposing ideas of what is falsely called knowledge (γνώσεως)." Radical dualism was a prime factor in the gnostic conceptual framework of the world.[3] Proper "knowledge" (γνῶσις) enabled people to see through the evil physical work of a "lower creator" and to perceive as their ultimate goal a return to the spiritual realm of the highest god, which was often depicted as the "Kingdom of Light." In the gnostic view the end (τέλος) of history was the dissolution of the physical world and the return of the human "sparks of light" to the Kingdom of Light.

The church has never completely escaped from these gnostic dangers. Manichaeism was an ancient gnostic heresy, while today various kinds of theosophical movements embrace tenants of Gnosticism. The sections of American society that embrace these beliefs include some elements of the New Age Movement.[4] The movement's frequent approach to the body is to demean it and finally to reject it.

Social scientists estimate that more then ten million Americans have participated in New Age activities that turn them inward toward their "psychic abilities" or "inner healing."[5] Specialists in "past life regression" assume that people have souls that existed in other human bodies in other times and places throughout history.[6] Tucker writes, "Most people I interviewed claimed that their power and knowledge is ultimately available to everyone."[7] New Age spirituality abandons the "evil" world and seeks answers from the "god within" by means of "mystical experiences."[8]

Those who have rejected their bodies are directed to the baptismal promises in 1 Peter 2:9–10. In Holy Baptism the Triune God not only cleanses our conscience (1 Pt 3:21), but also our *bodies*. In fact, our "bodies are washed with pure water" (Hebrews 10:22). In baptism both body and soul become a new creation (2 Cor 5:17) and even though outwardly the body wastes away, the baptized accept their bodies knowing that at the Second Advent of Christ they will receive glorified bodies (Phil 3:21).

The American Mind: Perfect the Body

Another, and much more popular response to the body, is to perfect it. Physical well-being has become a competitive goal of perfection, and any degree of abuse (steroids or other physical performance enhancers, obsessive exercise) or significant investment in exercise equipment is acceptable in achieving the goal.

Paul writes in 1 Corinthians 6:19, "Do you not know that your body is a temple of the Holy Spirit, who is in you, whom you have received from God?" A temple is not an object of worship but a place of worship. But in seeking to perfect the body American society encourages the worship of what is created rather than the Creator. Paul writes in Romans 1:25, "They exchanged the truth of God for a lie, and worshiped and served created things rather than the Creator."

In an article entitled "Beautiful Minds?" Michelle Tackla notes that a recent study attempts to demonstrate that cosmetic surgery boosts people's happiness.[9] Citing a study by the American Society of Aesthetic Plastic Surgery, there is "a very significant improvement in the quality of life at six months following surgery compared to the quality of life before surgery."[10] Even a partial list of options is impressive: rhinoplasty (fixing the nose); acne scar removal, sometimes called dermabrasion; liposuction (reduces the number of fat cells in the body); otoplasty (ear augmentation); breast augmentation; breast reduction; lip enhancement; and hair and tattoo removal.[11] The demand for cosmetic procedures jumped 44% in 2004 when almost 11.9 million surgical and nonsurgical procedures were performed in the United States. Liposuction remains the most popular surgical procedure for both men and women.[12]

Another element in this quest to perfect the body is an improper view of medicine. Stanley Hauerwas and Charles Pinches maintain that medicine in America "is fueled by the utopian presumption that illness can be cured or tamed by skill and science."[13] They argue that American society, to a large extent, forms people into compliant medical subjects and that most of us have become "good servants of the medical regime."[14] Medicine is more powerful and pervasive in our lives than the church ever was. In fact, in many American minds, medicine and science have replaced God. "For modern medicine was formed by a modern culture that forced upon medicine the impossible role of bandaging the wounds of societies that are built upon the premise that God does not matter."[15]

Medicine, viewed in the wrong way, functions as an insurance policy that gives people a sense that they will not have to come to terms with the reality of their own death. In this system the "high priests" are the doctors; the "temple attendants" are the medical technicians; "temples" are the hospitals; the "inspired text" is imparted by the medical community; and the eschatological goal is to escape death. The mantra is: "Medicine will perfect my body!"

Those who seek to perfect their bodies are called upon to "honor *God* with [their] bodies" (1 Corinthians 6:20), and not themselves. Medical care, eating healthy food, and exercising regularly are good, even godly habits (cf. 1 Tm 4:8). These are to be practiced, however, so that our bodies may be "living sacrifices, holy and pleasing to *God*" (Rom 12:1).

The Mind of Christ: Respect the Body

In the midst of a society that either rejects or seeks to perfect the body, the Mind of Christ (cf. 1 Cor 2:16) empowers another approach—

respect the body. Northrop Frye has stated this position in this way: "To steer some sort of middle course between the gnostic contempt for nature and the pagan adoration of it."[16] But how do we do this? One way, offered, tongue in cheek, is to encourage this prayer:

Lord, grant me the strength that I may not fall
Into the clutches of cholesterol.
At polyunsaturates I'll never mutter,
For the road to hell is paved with butter.
And cake is cursed, and cream is awful,
And Satan is hiding in every waffle.
Beelzebub is a chocolate drop,
And Lucifer is a lollypop.
Teach me the evils of hollandaise,
Of pasta and gobs of mayonnaise
And crisp fried chicken from the South.
Lord, if you love me, shut my mouth![17]

All of us have had the experience of being out of shape. Zippers start ripping out, buttons pop off, the car leans dangerously to one side when we get in. "Okay," we determinedly say, "I'm going to thin down." In the fresh enthusiasm of zeal we purchase new running shoes, join a local health club, and blow off the dust of that miserable diet book we bought five years ago. "I'm going to shave off thirty pounds!"

The very first day we start with a flash. We hit the road, running like we are on fire. We choke down dry toast, cottage cheese, sliced tomatoes, and a boiled egg. But then the holiday season rolls around and we fudge, then gorge. And when the urge to take care of our bodies comes over us, we just lie down quietly until the urge goes away. What is our problem?

Our problem is that our theology has a blind spot when it comes to proper stewardship of our bodies due to our neglect of the doctrine of creation. This has come about, in large part, because the church has ignored its Old Testament roots. In large part Platonism is to blame for the church's neglect of the body.[18] Plato held that there are two worlds: the visible, material world and the invisible, spiritual world. Because it is imperfect and a source of evil, the material world is inferior to that of the spiritual. Related to this dualistic view of the cosmos, then, is a dualistic view of people. Plato likens the body to a prison for the soul. The immortal soul is incarcerated in a defective body of crumbling clay. Salvation comes at death, when the soul escapes the body and soars heavenward to the invisible realm of the pure and eternal spirit. The widespread influence of Plato upon Christian thought can hardly be overestimated. But the Old Testament does not teach cosmological dualism (the belief that the created world is evil) nor anthropological dualism (soul versus body).

Genesis 2:7 states that Yahweh formed Adam from the dust of the ground and "breathed into his nostrils the breath of life, and the man became a living being (נֶפֶשׁ חַיָּה)." The נֶפֶשׁ is primarily a person's vitality, their life; it never denotes a separate part of a person. This means that people are a body-soul. They are not a soul or spirit which now inhabits a body and will at death forever desert the body. None of the Hebrew terms translated "soul" (נֶפֶשׁ) or "spirit" (רוּחַ) refers to the nonphysical part of a human being. In Hebraic thought, "soul" or "spirit" refers to the whole person of the individual as a living being. It stands for the person himself. Human beings live as souls; they do not "have" souls.[19]

The ramifications of these ideas are often overlooked because most Old Testament theologies begin with Yahweh's call to Abram in Genesis 12.[20] Unfortunately, the practice of regarding history as the chief point of orientation for the Old Testament, while marginalizing Yahweh's actions in, with, and for his creation, has governed its interpretation for the last one hundred years, if not longer.

The scholarship of Gerhard von Rad (1901–1971) is one of the main reasons why the historical paradigm governed the study of the Old Testament, while the larger realm of creation was relegated to the background and assigned a marginal status. In 1936, von Rad published "The Theological Problem of the Old Testament Doctrine of Creation."[21] In this essay, he demonstrates his great debt to Karl Barth, while Barth, for his part, postulated a dialectical theology that grew out of his antagonism between revelation and natural theology.[22]

Influenced by Barth, von Rad believed that creation "performs only an ancillary function ... It is but a magnificent foil for the message of salvation."[23] The Old Testament's focus is upon what Yahweh does in *history*, as distinct from what he may do in *creation*. As such, von Rad excluded creation as a central arena of Yahweh's concern and care. He identified as Israel's earliest creeds passages like Deuteronomy 6:20–24; 26:5–10; and Joshua 24:1–13 that supposedly were the nation's core confession. These texts say nothing about creation.

Von Rad's work became the foundation for the slogan "God's mighty deeds in history," which was taken up in the United States chiefly by George Ernest Wright. For Wright too, creation played a decidedly peripheral role in biblical thought; he called it "a handmaiden, a servant of history."[24] Wright's main thesis was that Yahweh is *sui generis* and has nothing in common with the gods and goddesses of Canaan. He wrote, "Israel was little interested in nature, except as God used it together with his historical acts to reveal himself and to accomplish his purpose."[25] More recently, Horst Dietrich Preuss affirmed that emphasis: "Yahwistic faith is primarily election faith on which is based faith in salvation." He supposed that creation theology, like the religious festivals, "belonged to the elements of the piety of a sedentary civilization which were later assigned to Yahwistic faith."[26] He saw creation as an add-on and therefore not central to Israel's *kerygma*.

This historical paradigm for interpreting Old Testament texts and understanding Israel's faith rests on four claims: (1) that history is a category distinct from creation and nature; (2) that Old Testament religion is grounded in history rather than the creation; (3) that Israel's religion in this regard was different from other ancient religions, which were grounded in creation; and (4) that the Old Testament's unique historical consciousness was an advance in the evolution of human thought. But these assumptions contain a fatal flaw: they all are based on the cultural worldview of modern Old Testament interpreters rather than the worldview of ancient Israel.[27]

The assumption that history and the creation are distinct categories of thought appears to depend most directly on the idealistic philosophical tradition as it was articulated by G. W. F. Hegel. As did the great idealists before him, Hegel divided the world into two metaphysically distinct orders, the spiritual and the material, and he used these dualistic categories to explain the history of religion. The oldest religions of the ancient Near East, according to Hegel, could be assigned to the material side of this ledger in that they identified God directly with the creation. The religion of Israel, by contrast, could be assigned to the spiritual side, since it separated Yahweh from the creation and connected him instead with humanity, spiritual individuality, and freedom, that is, with historical existence. In Israelite religion, according to Hegel, "man is exalted above all else in the whole creation,"[28] while "nature is represented as thus entirely negated, in subjection, transitory."[29]

Because of this marginalization of creation, the creation account in Genesis has customarily been identified as a prologue to what follows. Von Rad thought that the "pre-patriarchal history" in Genesis 1–11 was added last and derived "from a totally different sphere of culture and religion" than the indigenous Israelite sagas of the patriarchs and Moses, which followed.[30] Nahum Sarna's comments in the introduction to his Genesis commentary are representative: "The theme of Creation, important as it is, serves merely as an introduction to the book's central motif: God's role in history. The opening chapters are a prologue to the historical drama that begins in chapter 12."[31] Each of these interpreters clearly had a history-centered paradigm: creation is alien to, and the mere prologue for, the real historical religion of the patriarchs and Moses.

However, this dichotomy between spirit and matter is not part of the conceptual framework of the Old Testament. God created people as whole living beings with a physical body and soul or spirit. Moreover, God remains active in history as he preserves and redeems his people. Toward the end of his life, von Rad recognized this problem: "The Old Testament draws no such distinction between Nature and history."[32]

The formulations of von Rad, Wright, and others began to unravel in the 1970s. One reason for this dismantling was the work of James Barr, who wrote a book that sent seismic shocks throughout the Heilsgeschichte movement.[33] In it, he suggests that the etymological word studies upon which much of this interpretation had been based were methodologically weak. Brevard Childs also assisted in this deconstruction. In a series of studies, he made the case that reliance on history alone is an untenable approach to the Old Testament.[34] In addition, in 1971 Claus Westermann composed a seminal essay that argued for a more balanced view of creation in Old Testament theology.[35] He wrote: "The acting of God in creation and his acting in history stand in relation to one another in the Old Testament; the one is not without the other... Creation and history arise out of the same origin and move toward the same goal."[36]

Another voice in this growing chorus was that of Frank Moore Cross. In his influential book *Canaanite Myth and Hebrew Epic*,[37] Cross argued that Israel's faith is a combination of creational and redemptive ideas. Rather than posit an "either/or" between these two modes of expression, Cross offered a "both/and" approach. Yahweh is not just the enactor of historical deeds in Israel. He is also the one who ordered and commanded all of reality. *Redemptive acts have creational ends.*

More recently, Terence Fretheim has argued for not putting asunder what Yahweh has joined together; his concern for his creation and his actions in history.[38] According to Fretheim, the fact "that the Bible begins with Genesis, not Exodus, with creation, not redemption, is of immeasurable importance in understanding all that follows."[39] He points out that what Yahweh does in redemption is in the service of his endangered creation. For example, the deliverance of Israel is for the sake of all creation (Ex 9:16). What is at stake is Yahweh's mission for the world (Ex 9:29; 19:5). This means that Yahweh's redemptive activity on behalf of Israel is not an end in itself; it stands in the service of the entire creation.

All of this means that disregard for Yahweh's creation, so heavily dependent on the Hegelian dualism of spirit and matter, is antithetical to the faith of the Old Testament. Speaking about Yahweh in the language of "history" as opposed to "creation" is not being faithful to the biblical text. Rather, we must understand Yahweh's redemptive acts in history as his way to restore his creatures and bring about his new creation, which ultimately is in Christ (2 Cor 5:17; Gal 6:15; Rv 21–22). His work in creating the universe provides the foundation for his work in redemption. And what he does in redemption is to serve his eschatological goal for his corrupted, dying creation. The God of creation and the God of the Gospel are not two gods, but one. All three articles of the Creed confess one and the same God: Father, Son, and Holy Spirit.

In the incarnation of Jesus Christ, Yahweh joins creation to history in this most profound way. In the hypostatic union, the two natures in Christ continue in their integrity; his divine nature from eternity and his human nature, which he assumed when he was conceived by the Holy Spirit of the Virgin Mary.[40] From the moment of his conception on, Jesus is and will be forever both fully and true God and fully and true man.

Lutheran theology has long recognized that creation cannot and should not be relegated as a second-class doctrine. For example, in 1524 Andreas Karlstadt, one of Luther's companions, opposed the reformer by teaching that Christians must detach themselves from earthly, created things. In the framework of such a theology, Karlstadt taught that the Eucharist did not give an objective assurance of the forgiveness of sins because, as a part of this creation, it is unable to touch the depth of the soul. Luther refuted this divorce between creation and redemption in his writing *Wider die himmlischen Propheten von den Bildern und Sakrament*.[41] In this treatise, the reformer teaches that the Father works through the flesh of his Son to impart the Holy Spirit and new life. This is the fundamental means of his activity. In another context, Luther writes: "The Spirit cannot be with us in any other way than by physical things, such as the Word, the water [Baptism], the body of Christ [the Supper], and his saints on earth."[42] This is because "the body and flesh of Christ accord well with the Spirit; they even constitute the physical home of the Spirit, and by them the Spirit comes to others."[43]

Redemption is penultimate while a new creation is God's ultimate goal. This means, among other things, that redemption entails more than spiritual matters; it includes the healing of the body, the final resurrection, as well as the restoration of the entire inanimate universe.

Conclusions

Let's imagine that someone walks into your home, hands you the keys to a $75,000 Mercedes Benz and says, "Surprise, the car is all yours! Enjoy! One thing, though. It's an engineering marvel with a very sophisticated engine. It won't run on regular unleaded fuel. If you don't fill it with super unleaded, you'll eventually ruin the motor. Will you agree to use only the highest grade of fuel?"

I would agree. Wouldn't you? It would be unthinkable to ruin the car by not taking proper care of it.

But this is what many of the baptized are doing with their bodies. Granted, directed by God's word we don't intentionally reject or seek to perfect our bodies. But there are countless people who neglect their bodies. This is our blind spot. Many Christians believe the word "spiritual" means otherworldly piety. We have been taught that a "spiritual" person is one whose inner eyes are cast heavenward in prayer and contemplation, focusing on the joys of the life to come. To be "spiritual" implies that one is life-denying; it suggests communing with one's heavenly Creator by focusing upon the invisible realities and eternal mysteries of God's holiness. To live "spiritually" is often thought of in terms of passive detachment form this world, a transcending of the self to a higher, more sublime world. A "spiritual" person is really consumed with one agenda: "to win souls for Jesus." All other activity, such as that which seeks a healthy and fit body is inferior and lacking in priority.

The Old Testament views people as animated bodies rather than incarnated souls. For the Hebrews, spirituality did not mean turning inward; true piety was not simply the private nourishing of the virtues of one's soul. To be fully human meant to respect the body.

God has engineered a marvelous body for us. Our goal is to be available for Jesus Christ for the longest amount of time, with the greatest amount of energy, and the highest degree of emotional, mental, and spiritual well-being. True, this is but one spoke of the wheel, but deriving its power from the center, and in harmony with the other spokes, this good life begins in baptism and finds its ultimate fulfillment in the resurrection of the body in the New Jerusalem (Rv 21–22).

Endnotes

1 What follows is from the National Center for Health Statistics, National Health and Nutrition Examination Survey. Health, United States, 2002. Flegal et al. *JAMA*. 2002; 288: 1723–7.

2 Dave Moniz notes that the United States military has taken steps to confront its recruits who are raised on TV, video games, and the Internet. Drill sergeants have been known to call out-of-shape recruits "Nintendos" and "Segas" ("Drop and Give Me. . . Tougher Standards," *The Christian Science Monitor*, 91, no. 47 (1999): 1–2).

3 David N. Freedman, et. al. eds. *The Anchor Bible Dictionary* (New York: Doubleday, 1992), 2:1033–40.

4 A standard reference book for the movement is Shirley MacLaine's, *Dancing in the Light* (New York: Bantam, 1985).

5 As noted by James Tucker, "New Age Religion and the Cult of Self," *Society* 39, no. 2: 46–51.

6 This rejection of the body is encapsulated in this story told by Tucker: "A young woman frustrated with her inability to find a romantic partner met for almost three hours one evening with Jane, a specialist in 'past life regression' who operates out of a local health food store. Jane, who is single and in her early 50s, began the session by singing and ringing a bell. While continuing to sing, she ran her hands up and down the young woman's body. At one point, Jane stopped and explained what she had discovered. Apparently, the young woman lived as a man several centuries ago and had been fatally stabbed with a sword. Jane claimed that this wound remained with the woman for all of her subsequent lives. The pain in her heart was preventing her from achieving closeness with others. As a cure, Jane performed a healing exercise that involved blowing air on the client's chest" (Tucker, "New Age Religion and the Cult of Self," 47).

7 Tucker, "New Age Religion and the Cult of Self," 48.

8 Mariana Caplan offers a trenchant critique of the New Age Movement in "The Fate and Fallings of Contemporary Spirituality," *ReVision* 24, no. 2: 51–56.

9 Michelle Tackla, "Beautiful Minds?" *Dermatology Times* 24, no. 9, 78–81.

10 Tackla, "Beautiful Minds?" 78. For example, "Jana hated her nose. 'It was too big for my face,' Jana says. For her 16th birthday, Jana's parents agreed to pay for a rhinoplasty, or nose job ... Jana was happy with the results. 'I felt like I was attractive for the first time in my life'" (as noted by Melissa Abramowitz, "Facing the Facts about Cosmetic Surgery," *Current Health*, 27, no. 6, 19–21).

11 As noted by Abramowitz, "Facing the Facts about Cosmetic Surgery," 21.

12 As noted in *Dermatology Times*, 26, no. 3: 70.

13 Stanley Hauerwas and Charles Pinches, *Christians Among the Virtues: Theological Conversations with Ancient and Modern Ethics* (South Bend, IN: University of Notre Dame Press, 1997), 167.

14 Hauerwas and Pinches, *Christians Among the Virtues*, 167. For a series of essays that question the understanding of the body in modern medicine cf. *Troubled Bodies: Critical Perspectives on Postmodernism, Medical Ethics, and the Body*, ed. Paul Komersaroff (Durham, N.C.: Duke University Press, 1955).

15 Hauerwas and Pinches, 169.

16 Northrop Frye, *The Great Code: The Bible and Literature* (London: Routledge & Kegan Paul, 1982), 112–13.

17 Source unknown.

18 Cf. Marvin R. Wilson, *Our Father Abraham: Jewish Roots of the Christian Faith* (Grand Rapids: Eerdmans, 1989), 166–69.

19 Cf. William Dyrness, *Themes in Old Testament Theology* (Downers Grove, IL: InterVarsity Press, 1979), 85.

20 Cf. Rolf Rendtorff, "Some Reflections on Creation as a Topic of Old Testament Theology," in *Priests, Prophets, and Scribes: Essays on the Formation and Heritage of Second Temple Judaism in Honour of Joseph Blenkinsopp*, ed. Eugene Ulrich et al. JSOTSup 149 (Sheffield: JSOT Press, 1992), 204.

21 Gerhard Von Rad, *The Problem of the Hexateuch and Other Essays*, trans. E. Kitchen. (Edinburgh and New York: Oliver & Boyd, 1966).

22 Walter Brueggemann discusses the relationship between Barth and von Rad in *The Book That Breathes New Life: Scriptural Authority and Biblical Theology* (Minneapolis: Fortress, 2005), 83–84.

23 Von Rad, "The Theological Problem of the Old Testament Doctrine of Creation," in *The Problem of the Hexateuch and Other Essays*, 134. In his last book before his death, *Wisdom in Israel* (Nashville: Abingdon, 1972), von Rad gives a more prominent place to creation theology.

[24] George E. Wright, *God Who Acts: Biblical Theology As Recital* (London: SCM, 1952), 43. Wright's work is continuous with Karl Barth's rejection of "religion."

[25] Wright, *The Old Testament against Its Environment* (London: SCM, 1950), 9.

[26] Preuss, *Old Testament Theology*, 2 vols., trans. Leo Purdue (Louisville: Westminster John Knox, 1995), 1:237.

[27] Brueggemann discusses the zeitgeist of Barth and von Rad in which they developed their theology in *The Book That Breathes New Life*, 62–63.

[28] Hegel, *Lectures on the Philosophy of Religion*, trans. E. B. Speirs and Burdo Sanderson, (London: Routledge and Kegan Paul, 1962), vol. 2, 198.

[29] Hegel, *Lectures on the Philosophy of Religion*, vol. 2, 189.

[30] Von Rad, *"The Problem of the Hexateuch and Other Essays,"* 63–65.

[31] Nahum Sarna, *Genesis* (Philadelphia: The Jewish Publication Society, 1989), xiv.

[32] Von Rad, *"The Problem of the Hexateuch and Other Essays,"* 155.

[33] Barr, *The Semantics of Biblical Language* (Oxford: Clarendon Press, 1961).

[34] For example, Brevard S. Childs, *Biblical Theology in Crisis* (Philadelphia: Westminster, 1970), and *Biblical Theology of the Old and New Testaments: Theological Reflection on the Christian Bible* (Minneapolis; Fortress, 1992).

[35] Westermann, "Creation and History in the Old Testament," in Creation, trans. John J. Scullion (Philadelphia: Fortress, 1974); cf. also *Elements of Old Testament Theology*, trans. Douglas W. Scott (Atlanta: John Knox, 1982).

[36] Westermann, "Creation and History in the Old Testament," 24, 34.

[37] Cross, *Canaanite Myth and Hebrew Epic: Essays in the History of the Religion of Israel* (Cambridge, MA: Harvard University Press, 1973).

[38] Fretheim, *God and World in the Old Testament: A Relational Theology of Creation* (Nashville: Abingdon, 2005).

[39] Fretheim, *God and World in the Old Testament*, xix.

[40] The Athanasian Creed is especially concerned to explain the relationship between the divine and human natures in the one person of Jesus Christ, the second person of the Trinity. One may also see Martin Chemnitz, *The Two Natures in Christ*, trans. J. A. O. Preus (St. Louis: Concordia, 1971; originally published in 1578).

[41] *Against the Heavenly Prophets in the Matter of Images and Sacraments* (1525) WA 18:37–214; AE 40:73–223.

[42] Luther, *That These Words of Christ, "This Is My Body," Etc., Still Stand Firm against the Fanatics* (1527) WA 23.193:31–33; cf. AE 37:95).

[43] WA 23.195:3–5 (cf. AE 37:95).

Individualism and Community

Joel Biermann

Individualism as the Insistence on My Rights

> We hold these Truths to be self-evident, that all Men are created equal, that they are endowed by their Creator with certain unalienable Rights, that among these are Life, Liberty and the pursuit of Happiness.—That to secure these rights, Governments are instituted among Men, deriving their just Powers from the Consent of the Governed.

Admittedly, beginning with July 4, 1776 evidences an appalling lack of creativity and resourcefulness on the part of the essayist. Still, while there is hardly a more routine or predictable place at which to begin, the momentous words of Jefferson have become foundational to the American way of thought and life. As such, they are quite relevant to the "American mind." The declaration was ostensibly intended to proclaim the sovereignty of the fledgling New World democracy over against the tyranny of an Old World despot and government. The words, though, have become foundational to an even more treasured and far more practical ideal among residents of the American experiment. For the average American, the Declaration is not a manifesto of Enlightenment social theory or even a sacred national treasure. It is the enshrinement of his individual rights, the source and foundation of the American dream and the inspiration for the Bill of Rights. Every seven-year-old American child knows that to be human and American is to have rights—and above all else, the right to be free and happy. It is a given. It is axiomatic. The Declaration says so. It is more than a little outrageous and perhaps risky, therefore, to advance a position that assumes quite the opposite: there are no unalienable rights, there are no basic human rights, and there are no inherent rights of the individual—at least not in the sense that these "rights" are commonly understood in twenty-first century America.

The notion of humans with no rights was first imposed upon this writer one idyllic summer at a Lutheran camp in Nebraska. Conversing with a fellow counselor about the social evil of abortion, this hopelessly naïve and academically ill-equipped "pre-ministerial" student made the mistake of saying something like, "I think that it's important that we stand up for the rights of unborn babies." The statement sounded pure, basic, Christian, and American. And, besides, it was supported by the musician Phil Keaggy, whose song, "Who will Speak up for the Little Ones?" had sparked the conversation. That the subsequent events are still vividly remembered is testimony of their transformative and durative impact. "I don't believe any of us have any rights." My conversation partner delivered his broadside flatly and without flourish, but I was completely undone ... no rights!? How could that be? It was a disconcerting moment. I am sympathetic, then, to the discomfort and disorientation that may result from this paper's thesis. But it is a necessary thesis—more than ever as the tyrant of American colonial history has been thoroughly supplanted by today's lord and master: the sacred individual.

That American culture at the beginning of a new millennium is ego-centric about rights scarcely needs to be argued. The evidence is overwhelming and is encountered at virtually every turn on every day. In our culture—and in every culture tainted by even the smallest dose of western Enlightenment thought—it is taken for granted that each person has basic rights: the right to education, the right to health care, the right to tote a gun, the right to death with dignity, the right to vote, the right to worship or not, the right to own and sell property, the right to sue big business and win, the right to dream, the right to be free, and even the right to be right (even when I am wrong) and to have others compelled to agree that I am right. It is no exaggeration to observe that any given social issue or problem eventually devolves into a question of the exercise of these sacred individual rights. So, people enter into pitched battles over topics as diverse as mandatory seatbelt laws, a woman's right to choose, or discrimination inherent in job applications which provide only two mutually exclusive options by which an applicant is to describe her/his/(other?) "sex."

The debate over Missouri's stem-cell ballot initiative captured national attention in the fall of 2006 as a battleground in the ongoing war over the ethics of embryonic research. In essence, though, the real battle was about individual rights. The debate was a free-for-all over whose rights were to be upheld and whose trampled. Researchers claimed their right to do unencumbered scientific research. Those suffering from debilitating illness declared their right to every possible cure—real or imagined. Alarmed progressive voters insisted on their right not to be forced to conform to another's archaic code of morality; and yes, some voices even spoke up for the rights of the littlest and most easily overlooked humans in the debate—the embryos and blastocysts whose "right to life" would be sacrificed for the good of more mature, more familiar-looking humans who apparently matter more. But this is where the issue becomes particularly difficult for those who claim to follow in the train of Jesus Christ.

Whether the debate is abortion or the harvesting of embryonic stem cells, those opposed to the dehumanization of new human life and those who seek to protect the lives of the unborn will frequently ground their arguments in the notion of the rights of the children still in utero. Rhetorically, this may be a shrewd maneuver. It turns the argument on its head and exploits the fact that the sword of individual rights will cut very capably in both directions. What advantage is gained in the name of rhetoric or even apologetic, however, is gained at a dear cost ... but a cost that is rarely recognized or understood for the forfeiture that it is. What too many Christians learn too late is that any talk of personal rights will inevitably drive the individual to the center, by necessity displacing the one who alone has the right, to that position of authority and honor. To demand one's rights—yes, even to demand the rights of another—invariably ends with the individual self enthroned and both God and the neighbor deposed.[1]

It should be evident then, that the concern of this essay is not with a right granted by the state (as in the first ten amendments to the United States Constitution) or a right as a term to describe an obligation one may reasonably expect another to fulfill on his behalf (as in the mutual commitments of a business contract).[2] Rather, the problem is with the notion of the individual as a possessor of rights that he may claim and demand as an entitlement—a concept which leads to outcomes which are devastating to both active righteousness and passive righteousness alike. While it is granted that definitions that are more precise may safely retain the use of the term, I contend that in the popular understanding of the word "right" has been equated with the ideas of individual autonomy, the supremacy of the individual, and personal self-indulgence (usually masquerading as "self-actualization"). Such ideas are directly at odds with God's intentions for the right ordering of life in the horizontal realm (active righteousness) of this world *coram mundo*, and, it should be obvious, are the antithesis of faith in the vertical realm (passive righteousness) *coram deo*. Destructive outcomes such as these provide sufficient justification for the position of this paper—that for the sake of mankind, and for the sake of the individual man, it is best that every man be told that he has no rights.

But who would say such a thing? Even the church has difficulty surrendering to such a demanding, debilitating, and humiliating position. That the notion of personal rights has found a solid footing also in Christ's church is readily evident. Rick Warren famously began his best-seller with the bald assertion: "It's not all about you." This is an arresting thought, and appears to stand defiantly against the flood-tide of the surrounding culture's obsession with self. But, the remainder of the pastor's popular book betrays the high ideal of the opening sentence, and Warren cannot long maintain his radical thesis; he quickly and reassuringly retreats to the familiar formula: five steps to living the fulfilled life. The book *is* all about the reader. The individual triumphs once more. Still, sympathetic souls will find it difficult to fault Warren entirely. He is merely reflecting the culture he wants to engage, and more than that, he is reflecting the church that he seeks to represent.

Kurt Marquart made a typically astute observation (or is it a bitter complaint...?) in the context of discussing popular ideas about fellowship. He observed: "The individual comes first, the church second. Fellowship as human interpersonal relations defines the nature of the church rather than being derived from the prior nature of the church and understood therefore as common participation in the church's goods." This is followed by the relevant, trenchant observation:

> The results of such thinking, incubated for over a century in sentimentality and secularization, are today everywhere in evidence as a full-blown pathology: the church and her fellowship are expected to abdicate their own supernatural priorities, and to make themselves useful instead as emotional "support-groups" competitively servicing the "felt needs" of autonomous individuals/consumers, who in turn pursue their own inalienable right to self-determined "self-fulfillment." In such circumstances, and under the lash of pragmatism, it becomes in principle impossible to distinguish any longer between services and circuses, edification and exploitation, faithfulness and fraudulence, love and lunacy.[3]

Marquart very ably describes the status quo in much of what passes for Christianity, at least the sort of Christianity that captures magazine covers and garners prime-time interviews, the kind of Christianity—the kind of Lutheranism—that is typically proffered as "the church as it should be," making a "real difference" in the lives of "real people." What is relevant for this paper is the fact that this mischief, in all of its manifold variations and incarnations, also traces back to an assumption of the priority, that is the tyranny, of the individual and his sacred rights.

It has become a commonplace that "postmodern" people (exactly who and what this oft-referenced people might be, and whether such creatures exist, is another question altogether...)[4] value community and seek relationships. Such an interest would appear to offer a way to move the culture—or at least a few refugees of the culture—to recognize the futility and the error of asserting the idea of individual rights. To focus on community rather than on the self is a move in a more hopeful direction. Nevertheless, even this apparent turn from the self to the community is usually made in the interest of satisfying the felt needs of the individual and the community is reduced to playing the role of provider of the individual's desires. Individual rights continue to reign.

Still, the community is not a bad place to begin looking for a way out of the morass of rampant individualism and the clamor for the satisfaction of individual rights. But the community needs to be recognized as more than merely a gathering of like-minded individuals. The community exists with a life and a significance of its own—independent of the individuals who inhabit it. Such a community has history, purpose, and goals that serve to define its members and not vice versa. Such a community that exists as a unique and enduring entity makes claims on the individuals who live within its borders. In other words, the community comes first and the individual finds her place within the already established and functioning community.[5] The community claims the role of defining and shaping the individuals who make up the community. Hence, Hauerwas's memorable claim: "I want to be part of a community with the habits and practices that will make me do what I would otherwise not choose to do and then to learn to like what I have been forced to do."[6]

The critical point is that the individual is neither the center nor the *telos*. There is something bigger and more important than the individual with his list of rights waiting to be satisfied. The community and what the community is given to do matters more. The task of the individual, then, is not to supervise and tend the protection and fulfillment of his rights. Instead, his task is to find his place within the community. Rather than determining and defending his own rights, his responsibility is to learn to accept where he fits within the community and what tasks he needs to accomplish for the sake of those who live with him in that community. This is the concept that is at work when both Peter and Paul exhort their readers to "be in submission" to the appropriate authorities.[7] Literally, the people are to order themselves into the existing structure. They are to find their appropriate niche and fill it. The assumption, of course, is that the structure precedes and supersedes the needs and the rights of the individual. Also, one would hope that the community doing the shaping and supplanting the hegemony of the individual is actually a truthful community that rightly reflects the divine order.[8]

It should be clear, and not the least surprising, that the concept of natural law lurks in the immediate background of this discussion—that is, natural law as the description of the will of the Creator for his creation. Indeed, it is natural law, i.e., the "giveness" of God's creation and his law that guides that creation, which provides the best response to the individual's demand for the preservation of his rights. Instead of spending life defending one's rights, one should spend life ascertaining and then embracing the place that he has been given. Life is not about personal rights and the protection and cultivation of those rights in the hope that this will eventuate in self-fulfillment. Rather, life is the gift of the Creator who is the only source of the blessings (not rights) given to the individual, and the individual's fulfillment comes only when he conforms to the Creator's will and plan.[9]

It is worth noting that the contemporary slogans of "basic human rights" and the "inherent dignity of the person" both depend fundamentally on the existence and activity of a Creator. Despite recent, valiant efforts to ground the concept of natural law in the long processes of natural selection[10]—thus extracting the uncomfortable nuisance of God from one more aspect of contemporary life—the fact is that only a lawgiver outside of the system can provide any basis for talk of rights or dignity. Of course, this fact seems to be largely lost on most members of the wider culture who can dutifully endorse the tenets of Darwinism on the one hand and then glibly preach about the importance of human dignity and basic human rights on the other. The ugly and disturbing truth is that once God has been evicted from his place within human culture, then any sort of authoritative foundation for a discussion of good or right must be dismissed with him.

If Darwinism is correct, then a human being is nothing more than the latest iteration of so many chance meetings and coincident combinations of atoms. Having been reduced to being merely one particular collection of molecules—and nothing more, it is absurd that a human being should attempt to claim "inherent dignity" or "basic rights." The only dignity and the only rights that might still be claimed could be nothing other than those founded in the arbitrary preferences and sympathies of the wider society. Man invents the rights he likes and asserts the dignity that he wants. But as Nietzsche so forthrightly and frighteningly argued, once sentimental notions of inherent rights and attendant moral obligations have been excised and overcome, then all that is left by which to determine the right is the will to power. Rights are what someone, the one with the most power (the majority?), deigns to give to you. Few are willing to accept—much less endorse—this unpleasant outcome. Nevertheless, few seem willing to concede the fact that only recognition of a Divine lawgiver and accountability to that lawgiver that extends beyond the grave can avert this terror. Without a Creator, talk of human dignity and human rights is nonsensical.

The previous argument should not be construed as support for the notion that because God does indeed exist, so too do inherent human rights. It is merely offered by way of an observation that those who are prepared to argue favorably for human rights and human dignity must be willing to argue also for the existence of a God who creates and who will judge: no God, no rights. Still, the reciprocal is not true, and that God *is* does not necessitate the existence of basic human rights or validate their ruthless defense in the interest of self. Indeed, as the title of this essay indicates, it is the insistence on personal rights and a consequent entitlement mentality that are problematic. In the context of twenty-first century American culture, it is this author's contention that any talk of "rights" is liable to being construed so problematically.[11] As argued above, what God gives his creation is the privilege of bearing his image and the responsibility of serving the rest of creation. It is not a matter of rights, but a matter of gifts freely bestowed by the Creator and gratefully received by the creature.

To see one's life in the context of one's responsibilities to the rest of the creation is the fundamental point. Nature (or creation) does not bestow rights on the individual; rather the Creator graces the person with the gift of life, the gift of salvation, and the responsibility to care for the surrounding creation. While sin and its consequences infect and pervert the Creator's intentions for his creatures, the plan is still in effect, and the creature's purpose remains what it was at the outset. Man exists to serve the creation. Man lives for the good of the neighbor. Luther emphasized the implications of this arrangement with memorable intensity in his 1523 essay, "Temporal Authority: To What Extent It Should Be Obeyed."[12] Not without cause, this monograph is usually referenced in regard to Luther's teaching on the two realms or areas of God's activity in this world. But, along the way to establishing the distinction between God's work in the left hand realm from his work in the right hand realm, Luther delivers the coup de grace to any lingering idea of individual rights. Even whatever privileges or rights that had been granted by the state are snatched away from the individual who bears the name of Christ. "A Christian," Luther insists, "should be so disposed that he will suffer every evil and injustice without avenging himself; neither will he seek legal redress in the courts but have utterly no need of temporal authority and law for his own sake."[13] Luther reaches this challenging conclusion after considering and zealously applying Christ's instruction in the Sermon on the Mount: "Do not resist evil" (Mt 5:39). Still, the need to care for the neighbor brings an interesting twist to Luther's counsel:

> On behalf of others, however, he may and should seek vengeance, justice, protection, and help, and do as much as he can to achieve it. Likewise, the governing authority should, on its own initiative or through the instigation of others, help and protect him too, without any complaint, application, or instigation on his own part. If it fails to do this, he should permit himself to be despoiled and slandered; he should not resist evil, as Christ's words say.[14]

For the sake of the neighbor, one may claim a right to protection and justice under the law—but not for oneself. For self, all claims are barred ... at least, that's the way that Luther reads it.

The astute practitioner of casuistry will immediately begin to wonder about all manner of extenuating circumstances. Luther anticipates and addresses the most viable:

> You may ask, "Why may I not use the sword for myself and for my own cause, so long as it is my intention not to seek my own advantage but to punish evil?" Answer: Such a miracle is not impossible, but very rare and hazardous.[15]

Luther tries to bolster his argument by appealing to Samson as an example of one who while furthering his own cause, "did not do so in order to avenge himself or to seek his own interests, but to serve others and to punish the Philistines."[16] That Luther can suggest the dubious (indeed, ironically unconvincing!?) example of Samson as one who serves self for the sake of others is perhaps the greatest evidence of all that such an occurrence is truly miraculous with no positive example readily available. Nevertheless, with or without Samson, Luther's point is clear—the Christian has no right to claim his own rights. He can only throw himself on the mercy of God and trust the goodness of others. Luther leaves the follower of Christ bereft of rights.

In a world obsessed with the attainment, protection, and fulfillment of individual rights, there is something at once sublime and elegant about the simplicity of Luther's position. While majorities and minorities and individuals noisily, ceaselessly, and repugnantly insist that everyone else attend to their rights, Christians simply repudiate the whole idea. They refuse to play the game. This is profoundly beautiful. And, it should be obvious, people who live this way will stand apart from the crowd not only as rare and different, but also as beautiful and attractive. One could scarcely imagine a more arresting witness to the community than a group of people who refuse to stand on their rights either individually or collectively. Luther was convinced that this was no utopian ideal, but was the enacted reality for the individual and the community called by Christ.

The twenty-first century congregation striving for relevance and vitality would do well to consider the challenge of living without rights.

Once the premise has been granted, many practical questions immediately present themselves. Can a congregation demand its right to release time for the education of its children? Is it wrong for a congregation to pursue its right to legal redress over a property dispute? Should a Christian complain to the manager and expect compensation when a restaurant spoils his order and his evening? What is the difference between helping another person do his task well and standing on individual rights to have the task done to his own level of satisfaction? How does a Christian who has renounced his rights not become a doormat to any and every ne'er-do-well who comes along? These and countless other questions resist easy, one-size-fits-all solutions. Yet, in the course of faithful dialogue and reflection, useful answers will come.

The argument of overriding concern is that the whole notion of individual rights be challenged and subverted. At least beginning with the church, this must be the goal. Both the Christian and the congregation will be transformed when an attitude of rights and entitlements is replaced with a gracious posture of humble reception of gifts that are not deserved and mercy that is not expected. Not only is this the right posture when one comes before his Lord, it is also the right posture for one who wants to carry the truth of his Lord into a world consumed and infatuated with the pursuit of rights. The individual Christian knows that he doesn't need rights. He has Christ. He has the community of Christ's church. In possession of all that he could ever need, why denigrate it with a tawdry insistence on personal rights? Let the American mind pursue the course of individual rights; the mind of Christ delights in a reality infinitely more beautiful.

Endnotes

1 Gustaf F. Wingren, "Justification by Faith in Protestant Thought," *Scottish Journal of Theology* 9 (December 1956): 374–383. Especially relevant is Wingren's argument on page 376.

2 C.S. Lewis, "We Have No Right to Happiness," in *God in the Dock: Essays on Theology and Ethics*, ed. Walter Hooper (Grand Rapids: Eerdmans, 1970), 317–322. Among the keen insights of this short essay, Lewis offers this observation: "A right to happiness doesn't, for me, make much more sense than a right to be six feet tall, or to have a millionaire for your father, or to get good weather whenever you want to have a picnic" (318).

3 Robert D. Preus, ed. *Confessional Lutheran Dogmatics*, Vol. 9, *The Church and Her Fellowship, Ministry, and Governance*, by Kurt E. Marquart, (Fort Wayne, IN: The International Foundation for Lutheran Confessional Research, 1990), 45–46.

4 Cf. Stanley Hauerwas, *Sanctify Them in the Truth: Holiness Exemplified* (Nashville: Abingdon Press, 1998), 191.

5 This line of thought was classically and influentially developed in Alasdair MacIntyre's, *After Virtue: A Study in Moral Theory*. (Notre Dame: University of Notre Dame Press), 1981.

6 Stanley Hauerwas, *In Good Company: The Church as Polis*, (Notre Dame: University of Notre Dame Press, 1995), 75.

7 Cf. Romans 13:1-7; Corinthians 11:3–16, 14:34; Ephesians 5:22–23, I Timothy 2:11; Titus 2:5; and I Peter 3:1 (*hypotage*).

8 Cf. George A. Lindbeck, *The Nature of Doctrine: Religion and Theology in a Postliberal Age*. (Philadelphia: Westminster Press, 1984).

9 The idea of freedom as conformity to the will of the Creator is capably argued by Reinhard Hütter. Cf. Reinhard Hütter, "(Re-)Forming Freedom: Reflections 'After *Veritatis Splendor*' On Freedom's Fate in Modernity and Protestantism's Antinomian Captivity." *Modern Theology* 17, no. 2 (April 2001): 117–161. Clearly, the idea of vocation is also of critical importance, but a discussion of this topic lies beyond the scope of the present paper.

10 Cf. Marc Hauser, *Moral Minds: How Nature Designed Our Universal Sense of Right and Wrong* (New York: Ecco, 2006).

11 Of course, the author also recognizes that serious and faithful ethical thinkers in other contexts have safely used the term "rights" to convey ideas altogether in agreement with the thesis of this essay which denies the existence of rights. The critical point, naturally, is one's definition of rights. Noteworthy is Bonhoeffer's discussion of rights. In his *Ethics* he argues: "And indeed in the rights of natural life it is not to the creature that honour [sic] is given, but to the Creator. It is the abundance of His gifts that is acknowledged. There is no right before God, but the natural, purely as what is given, becomes the right in relation to man. The rights of natural life are in the midst of the fallen world the reflected splendour [sic] of the glory of God's creation. They are not primarily something that man can use for his own interest, but they are something that is guaranteed by God Himself." (Dietrich Bonhoeffer, *Ethics*, trans. by Neville Horton Smith [Touchstone, New York, 1995], 150.) Later, Bonhoeffer puts an even tighter clamp on the definition of rights: "The only human and natural rights are those which derive from Christ, that is to say, from faith" (356). With thanks to Adam Clark for helpfully calling the author's attention to these passages.

12 *Luther's Works*, Eds. Jaroslav Pelikan and Helmut T. Lehmann. American Edition, 56 vols. (St. Louis and Philadelphia: Concordia Publishing House and Fortress Press, 1958-86), Vol. 45, 73–129.

13 Ibid., 101.

14 Ibid., 101

15 Ibid., 104

16 Ibid.

Leopoldo A. Sánchez M.

Individualism, Indulgence, and the Mind of Christ: Making Room for the Neighbor and the Father

Theology done in North America must deal with the broader western shift to the individual in his human and historical complexity. How does the church proclaim Jesus Christ to those who value individual reason (modernity) and, above all, individual perspective (postmodernity) and voice (post-colonialism)? Her witness will discern between a relatively positive "individualistic impulse" in society that foments creativity and a strong work ethic, and a sinful "impulsive individualism" which upholds the self to the exclusion of the neighbor. In our society, the church's call to behold Christ the Servant and embody servanthood can channel self-indulgent individuals into persons who make room for the other. Care must be taken, however, not to equate the need for some indulgence with selfishness. An overworked North American society will also benefit from the church's call to behold Christ the Son and embody his openness to leave the crowds to find refreshment and rest from the busyness of life in prayer-dialogue with God the Father.

Like other "isms," the term individualism seeks to embody a world-view, thought system, and way of life that makes the individual its central concern or driving force. In the modern West, Descartes's *cogito ergo sum* has often served as an indicator of the monumental shift from a theo-centric to an anthropocentric view of the universe. In the post-Cartesian West, we have inherited a point-of-no-return that demands theology—even a theocentric one—take seriously in its reflection the turn to the human subject in his psychological complexity, historicity, and social location. Do you care about *me*?

I.

Theological approaches "from below" that move within the realm of the human and the historical are not uncommon today. A Christology "from below," for example, takes as its starting point the man Jesus of Nazareth, his historicity and social location, his life in the Spirit, and/or his words and deeds in salvation history. Such an approach might follow Christological and ecclesiological trajectories. On the side of Christology proper, the move "from below" might work within the *ordo cognoscendi* (order of knowledge), in which Jesus is fully acknowledged as Savior, Lord, and God on the basis of his works for us—especially in light of his resurrection. Such an approach makes abundantly clear that there is no access to the divine Logos apart from this man Jesus of Nazareth and his deeds.[1] I come to know Jesus as God because he saves me.

Perhaps more important for our discussion, the move "from below" highlights, on the ecclesiological side, what we have in common with Christ, namely, a human life and history. Jesus is our brother, like us in every way "yet without sin" (Heb 2:16–17, 4:15). He is the *primogenitus*, the firstborn among many brethren, the one from the race of Adam who goes before us unto death, the firstfruits of our resurrection who restores us to the image of God lost by Adam (Rom 8:29–30, Heb 3:10–18, 1 Cor 15:20–23, 45–49). In a pneumatological Christology one could say, for example, that the Son and the sons share in common their anointing with the Spirit and their being raised from the dead by the Father according to the Spirit.[2] To use western Christological categories, the incarnate Word shares what is uniquely his—his *gratia personalis* (or in more personal terms, his Spirit)—with his members as head of the church (*gratia capitis*). The receiver and bearer of the Spirit becomes the giver of the Spirit to others.[3] A theology of the Christian life might argue that the same Spirit in whom Christ struggled against the anti-kingdom, proclaimed the Word of God, and prayed to his Father shapes the church's life and mission after Christ's own.[4] We can then speak of the Christoform character of the church's mission and the Christian life.

Nowadays, borderlands (i.e., poor and marginalized) communities will also appeal to Jesus' social location in their missiological and ethical reflection. For example, Latino theologians in North America might point to Jesus' Galilean social location to speak of the incarnation in terms of God's self-identification with the poor and marginalized.[5] This approach "from below" in turn allows for a holistic or integral approach to missions that does not simply think of the "lost" as the atheist, agnostic, secularized "non-believer" of the modern West (or the North Atlantic) but also as the "non-committed," religious, and often believing "non-being" of the two-thirds world outside (or inside!) first-world countries.[6] Missions in Galilee will require an accompanying ethical commitment to God's concern for the *totus homo*, soul and body, and specifically a priority of love towards not only the neighbor "in general" but the neediest neighbors among us—what some in Latin America have called a non-exclusive "preferential option for the poor."[7]

These reflections are meant to point out that there is no escaping the deep yearning of many in the West for a message that values the turn to the human subject and, therefore, resonates with and addresses concrete human needs and hopes. The modern move to the centrality of the human and the historical has not escaped postmodernity, which assumes and affirms an individual's perspective on all things. In between cartoons, PBS reminds me to make room for my child's creative angle on things. The ad goes, "It's all how you look at it." I am asked implicitly to affirm my child's individual perspective and to allow it to flourish into some creative output. Without minimizing the danger of praising such individuality in American education to the detriment of building a learning community and solidarity among students, creating a space for each person to think for himself and provide his take on the world fosters creativity and possibility. This is perhaps the kind of individuality that has driven some to compose a unique symphony or crack a tough murder case, and others to solve a difficult math problem or craft a persuasive argument.

To vilify postmodernism for its potential danger to foster rampant relativism on the "truth" is to see with one eye, to miss its potential contribution to take seriously the turn to the subjective and the perspectival in the interpretation of reality. It is entirely possible for two confessional Lutherans from two different cultures, in two different parts of the world, to look at the same biblical text with reverence and read two distinct yet faithful accounts of the truth which points to Christ. Does not the Holy Spirit lead the church—catholic as it is—continually into the truth, into a deeper and ever fresh hearing and speaking of the words of Christ, in her own and for her own situation and time? The critical need for discerning the spirit aside, the affirmation of perspectives can follow from the humble recognition that God's truth is rich and inexhaustible, ever so deep that the well never runs dry.

The modern shift to the human subject has not escaped post-colonialism either, which reclaims and creates a space for an individual's once-silenced voice to be heard. There is, of course, a profound awareness nowadays—above all, among marginalized groups—of the dynamics of power in the creation of perspective. If the modern turn to objective human reason is now under the eye of the postmodern watchdog, the postmodern turn to the perspectival is under the eye of the post-colonial watchdog lest perspective becomes the exclusive sphere of the powerful.

We find an example of post-colonial thought in singer/songwriter and politician Rubén Blades's deconstruction of the colonial enterprise in the Americas. Blades sings of formerly colonized peoples as trained parrots who are called to dis-cover (uncover or unmask) their own history and identity. With some relief, Blades thinks about how "I almost learned to forget what *I* was. Truth is never convenient for a master's plan."[8] The emphasis is on "almost." I am asked to think for myself in order to find myself. There is an affirmation of individuality, the kind that moves courageous individuals to "think outside of the box" and risk speaking their mind in the face of conformity or opposition: freedom fighters, civil rights activists, and—dare we say—preachers of the Word. Post-colonial thinking calls for a reconstruction of history "from below," from the underside, from the voices of the colonized and silenced. Interestingly, and precisely to make room for the voices, Mexican-American essayist Richard Rodríguez has expressed his discontent with a complete *relectura* (re-reading) of United States history from the underside because it alone cannot face courageously the mixed bag of treasures and prejudices that have also played a part in the lives of Blacks, women, and immigrants up to this day.[9] Historian Daisy Machado writes that our churches need to face the historic curses of being marginalized by Spanish-Catholic and English-Protestant missionaries to understand what it means for Mexican-Americans to be seen as less than Mexican to the Mexicans and less than North American to the North Americans.[10] Machado speaks for herself to find herself. So do Rodríguez and Blades.

II.

Along with the modern, postmodern, and post-colonial turns to individual reason, perspective, and voice respectively, there has also been a move in the West towards an understanding of humans not simply as individuals who exist and function in and by themselves but more fully as "persons" who exist and live with and for another. Humans are social beings who find fulfillment in their relations or, better yet, are fully human through their relations. Individuality is then not an abstract starting point but concretely a product of one's relations. "She is daddy's girl!" "He is God's child!" Such a relational approach is evident, for example, in Jewish philosopher Martin Buber's "I-Thou" focus on humans as dialogical creatures, made by God to be addressed by others, and addressed to others.[11]

In contemporary theology, relational ontologies also posit the priority and ultimacy of the person in ecclesiology, Trinitarian discourse, and ethics. Orthodox theologian John Zizioulas, for example, sees the fullness of being human in being a member of the church gathered around the Eucharist.[12] To use his language, the biological hypostasis (being) is fulfilled in the ecclesial hypostasis. Ontologies of personhood in Trinitarian studies have arisen in response to real or perceived "theisms" that portray God as a self-enclosed (individualistic!) being, and in particular as one who appears to be unaffected by and unresponsive to human suffering. For Moltmann (Germany), Boff (Brazil), and LaCugna (United States), the perichoretic relations among the persons of the Trinity—their being with and in each other—in the immanent and/or the economic realm have served as a model for communion in church and society which should ideally lead to ecumenical and political commitments in favor of inclusion and justice at various levels.[13]

Whatever one thinks of the ecclesial and political options per se, one should note that, generally speaking, the shift to the "person" in European theology has generally been a *sine qua non* of doing theology "after Auschwitz"—an approach that takes seriously God's dwelling with the crushed and the lowly in the midst of suffering and the church's commitment to stand on the side of the suffering. In Latin America, Jon Sobrino once said that theology in the region was actually being done "in Auschwitz."[14] The point was to highlight the context for doing theology, namely, a situation of mass suffering due to political repression, economic exploitation, and human rights violations.

In the North American situation, open theism has attempted to handle the prospect of an individualistic, apathetic view of God, through the not-so-unproblematic combination of divine self-limitation and human freedom. The so-called classical theistic theology that safeguards divine transcendence clearly preserves God's distinction from creation but might offer less by way of a God who listens to and is moved to act by our prayers.[15] The problem lies in that both forms of theism are substantialisms that do not arrive at the story of salvation, the narrative of divine persons in merciful communion with creatures.

Taking a different trajectory, Newyorican theologian Samuel Soliván has tried to do the same by calling for a recovery of *orthopathos* in a comfortable and individualistic North American church that often uses *orthodoxy* talk and *orthopraxis* talk as attempts at self-justification in order to avoid involvement in concrete forms of solidarity with the suffering.[16] Soliván finds theological ground for the church's *orthopathos* in the Son's self-identification with the suffering in his incarnation. The point is not that a suffering misery-loves-company God can best relate to us in our suffering, but rather that the Son has shown solidarity with suffering humanity in his humiliation and poverty and, therefore, the church is called to do the same in the world today.

In a broader historical context, the French and American revolutions, as well as the rise in the West of industrialized and market-capitalist societies, have been tied to that "individualistic impulse" which fosters independent thinking and acting in the crafting of one's self-identity and vision for society. One might say this individualistic impulse—or does an impulse towards individuality sound freer from selfish connotations?—has been present in unnumbered criticisms of the status quo, deadly conformism, and a fatalistic worldview, especially if there is a sense that fresh thinking, progress, and certain political and economic freedoms are being denied. Having said that, there is the real danger of moving from what may be seen as a relatively benign "individualistic impulse" to an "impulsive individualism," an idolatrous concern for the self to the exclusion of the other.

In the inescapable shift to the human today, the Lutheran tradition hardly fails to take into account our *incurvatus in se* condition that leads us to turn apparent blessings like "freedom" and "capital" into idols which are used or function in ways that leave little or no room for the neighbor. One can hardly forget Luther's exhortation to the justified to use their freedom in Christ to serve others: "A Christian is a perfectly free lord of all, subject to none. A Christian is a perfectly dutiful servant of all, subject to all."[17] Or recall Luther's catechesis, in his criticism of idolatry, against acquiring money and possessions without any concern for the needy.[18] Whenever our freedom and capital take the place of the one true God in our lives, our neighbor will suffer from our idolatry. Conversely, whenever our freedom and capital are placed in service to our neighbor, we promote their well-being and, by doing so, do the will of God and honor the Creator of us all. Attempts to rediscover what Luther and the Confessions have to say on vocation and active righteousness signal an attempt to deal seriously with the question of the other; of our God-given responsibilities to live in a right relationship with others.[19]

Indulgence is defined in largely negative terms as the gratification of one's desires or whims, allowing one to have what he wants—not necessarily what he needs. It is the stuff that gives rise to spoiled kids at home and greedy CEOs in big companies. We have here a malign form of individualism, which in the North American context is often played out in a selfish appropriation of personal freedom and the pursuit of happiness. In general, this worldview is known in the classical philosophical sense as ethical hedonism, namely, the idea that pleasure (or happiness) is the ultimate good and that every act must aim at maximizing it. Even though hedonism may actually allow for preferred pleasures to be oriented towards the other, it is nevertheless most often associated exclusively with self-gain. An outstanding question is whether pleasure and happiness—whatever that is—is or should be the only, or even the greatest, value and goal in life.

Various theological resources can be deployed to put out the hedonistic fire; above all, is the church's call to and embodiment of servanthood. More radically, can we simply elevate servanthood to the position of highest goal and value in life? We think of the life of Christ, the suffering Servant, who "came not to be served but to serve" (Mk 10:45). So the Christian—to use Peter's words—"should follow in his steps," suffering all things for the sake of his neighbor (1 Pt 2:21). A Christology "from below" is well-equipped to affirm that the same Spirit in whom the Son is anointed as Servant now shapes the church's life so that she too might make room for the neighbor. Most powerful is Paul's ethical use of the mystery of the incarnation in the famous Christological hymn in Philippians. The passage speaks of the church's sharing in the mind of Christ. In his humiliation, Christ Jesus, "though he was in the form of God, did not regard equality with God as something to be exploited, but emptied himself, taking the form of a slave [or servant]" (Phil 2:6-7).

The mind of the servant Christ forms and guides the church's own thinking and living in the world: "Do nothing from selfish ambition or conceit, but in humility regard others as better than yourselves. Let each of you look not to your own interests, but to the interests of others. Let the same mind be in you that was in Christ Jesus" (Phil 2:3–5). The Holy Spirit does not simply have us look to Jesus "out there" in order to follow him, but actually shapes Christ "in here" (in our hearts and minds) so that our lives in service to others mirror Christ's own humility and self-giving. Selfishness meets selflessness. Self-indulgence meets self-giving. The North American mind meets the mind of Christ.

III.

We might, however, ask whether appeals to self-giving and selflessness actually work in the North American context. There might be deeper reasons that drive North Americans to become indulgent. In a recent trip to Panama, a neighbor gave me his take on life in the United States: "In Latin America, people work to live; in the United States, people live to work!" An outsider's perspective is often quite helpful. A quick look at T.V. infomercials or print ad appeals to become richer, more beautiful, and healthier are often pitched as well-deserved prizes or investments for hard-working people who never have time for themselves or their families. Although I was raised in Central America, I have lived and work in the United States long enough to resonate with the pitch. What is wrong with being pampered after a hard day at work? Why be a "sucker" who lets the company suck the life out of you? If I were to allow such "suffering"—let's say, even for the sake of the Gospel!—with no escape in view, am I not becoming a sort of masochist? Am I not denying myself ways to make room for myself and perhaps even my neighbor?

Selfishness and indulgence might not always go together.[20] Most parents will feed their children, change their diapers, and take care of them in times of sickness for no other reason than their deep love for them. They are selfless. Indeed, most parents will give their lives to save their children. Are we husbands to tell a hard-working (and even over-worked) mom in North America that she does not deserve a spa-treatment or a night out to a nice restaurant once in a while? More to the point: should she not get what she wants here and there? Extolling the virtues of servanthood at this point will sound out-of-touch—or just plain stupid—given the reality of the situation at home.

North Americans are too focused on getting results and dividends in an efficient and timely manner, but often at the expense of their human resources. Back in the days of the Panama Canal Commission (PCC), my father's boss—to use popular language, a *gringo*—in the Occupational Health & Safety Division used to focus on the importance of safety standards at work for the sake of efficiency in Canal operations. The message: "If you get injured and die, you cost the Canal time and money." When my father returned to the church after a long time away from the Lord, I attended one of his safety training sessions during a vacation. In a sort of defiant take on safety against the predominant view, my father—a committed Christian layman—told a crowd of Panamanian workers that safety was not ultimately an economic problem. It was not an issue of productivity and efficiency. It was a moral issue! He spoke to the workers about the recent death of an underwater repairman—one of the most dangerous jobs in the Canal—who never made it home to his family. He imprinted in their minds the image of the parked car in the lonely lot, the car whose owner was not coming back to drive it to see his wife and children. The message came out completely different: "If you get injured and die, you can't be there to take care of your family!"

In a context where it appears that the individualistic impulse has created a strong work ethic and, negatively speaking, "people live to work," one must be open to the idea that a measure of indulgence might not be necessarily the child of egoism. There is a real need behind the drive to rest and be refreshed. Perhaps there is a positive form of protective indulgence or concern for the self that serves as a way out of insanity, an attempt to escape from the ridiculously high demands of a materialistic culture where productivity and economic success are often valued at the expense of the worker. Maybe a measure of indulgence serves us to achieve a healthy balance in life between paid work proper and other vocations that also require attention. Should we imagine that there is a moral dimension to indulgence that prevents the dignity of the human from getting lost in the production line?

One often hears of speakers who talk about self-care. The point is usually that unless you take care of yourself you cannot really take care of others. In these talks, one often gets the sense that overworked people have a right to be indulgent. Supposedly, hard-working people deserve to get something they want. They have earned the freedom to make some choices. Without minimizing the real concern for refreshment behind these attitudes, one should also realize that self-indulgence is in some ways a commodity that North Americans can afford. In a culture that values choice and is given to excesses, indulgence becomes another way to exercise one's freedom to consume and possess. By contrast, there are hard-working people in many parts of the world, and many in these United States too, who simply cannot afford indulgence. Those who are better off and talk about taking care of self cannot but sound selfish by comparison. A little or a big indulgence might be a pragmatic way of relief. But there is simply no permanent rest and refreshment in a little indulgence. Where then do we go?

A better theological resource for the weary than "getting pampered a little" can be seen in another dimension of Christ's life, namely, his prayer-dialogue with the Father.[21] At times, there are crowds waiting to be healed, waiting to be served. Should not Christ drop everything and take care of their problems? But Christ leaves the crowds and spends time in prayer-dialogue with his Father (Lk 5:15–16). Here we have the other side of servanthood, namely, sonship.[22] We are so busy doing our work—in the worst sense, for ourselves; in the best sense, for our neighbor—that we do not have time to be still and act as children who talk to and hear their loving Father. The crowds call for our help, via e-mail, via cell phone, etc. There is no end to the requests. We are called to give our lives in the service of others. So is Christ.

But is it not remarkable—at least to people who are busy rushing all the time—that Christ does not let his service to the neighbor take over his prayer-dialogue with the Father? How does the church offer today's weary an opportunity to enter this holy space where they can hear and respond to the word of the heavenly Father?

How does one find refreshment and rest in God in the midst of a busy people? It will be more difficult to the extent that our churches in North America are run like businesses. What church does not have set working and worship hours? This is not bad, especially for pastors with families. Yet the practice is somewhat unsettling for someone like me who grew up in Latin America where a few churches are open for people to stop by on their way to and from work to hear Mass and pray—on a good day, this translates into hearing from and praying to the Word of God. A space to rest in God before and after work. How provocative! Could it be that churches no longer lend themselves to being houses of prayer, places of retreat, and oases in a desert that tempt us to lose ourselves in our work? Admittedly, church workers are often too busy in administrative work or raising funds for projects to spend quality time with the sheep or the strangers—much less with the Father. It is not uncommon for sheep to follow their pastor's example.

The question still remains for pastors, our sheep, and the community that surrounds our parishes and mission fields: how do worn-out people leave the crowds to hear and respond to the Father? Different answers will come. However, at times, it will be okay to do nothing—to rest, literally—to sit down, be still, prevent work from becoming our god, and actually live by faith as if the world does not ultimately depend on us or our work but on the Creator. Along with God's command to work—Luther reminds us—God commands the Sabbath: "We worship God also when we rest; indeed there is no greater worship of God than this."[23] A space literally to rest in God. How provocative!

In the United States today, while being a servant and embodying servanthood serves as a good antidote against an unhealthy drive for self-service, being a child who spends time in prayer-dialogue with the Father leads overworked servants to find rest in a loving God who addresses them as persons with his word, listens to them in prayer, and then sends them off to do their work with renewed insight and boldness.

Questions for Reflection

1. We have made a distinction between a relatively positive "individualistic impulse" and a sinful "impulsive individualism." How are these forms of individuality manifested among the people whom you serve in your congregation and community? What are some ways in which you can make individuality a means to the end of serving the neighbor?

2. In a society where the turn to the human subject is valued, are there some ways in which the church worker can make room for indi-

vidual reason, perspective, and voice in the life of a congregation? How do we foster a bold ministerial use of reason, perspective, and voice that is not only captive to but also confident in the Word of God as the answer to our deepest human sufferings and hopes?

3. The apostles chose deacons to devote themselves to prayer and the ministry of the Word (Acts 6:4). Lutherans dedicate more time and effort to the proclamation of the Word as a means of grace than to prayer as a response to the Word. This is justified. And yet the apostles still were devoted to prayer. What are some concrete ways you might consider to make room in your life for prayer? Are there areas of your ministry in which you are being overworked, and for which you are perhaps not really needed that take away from time to both hear the Word of God and pray to him? Who else could help you do the work you are not absolutely needed for? How might making room for prayer-dialogue with the Father before and after work change your schedule, ministry, and family life?

4. Well-known is the monastic motto *Ora et Labora* (Pray and Work). Luther was critical of monks who spent too much time praying to please God but not enough time fulfilling a vocation in the world to serve their poor neighbor. Perhaps, today we have the opposite problem: we live in a society where people spend too much time at work and give up their time with the Father. How does your congregation become an oasis of refreshment in a society filled with weary and overworked people? What are some concrete ways in which you, the church worker, might communicate intelligibly to and embody for the people in the congregation and the surrounding neighborhood that the church is a place for refreshment?

Endnotes

1 In a sermon for Trinity Sunday, Luther writes: "The Scriptures gradually and beautifully lead us to Christ; first revealing him to us as a man, then as the Lord of all creatures, and finally as God. Thus we are successfully led to the true knowledge of God. But the philosophers and the wise men of this world would begin at the top and so they have become fools. We must begin at the bottom and gradually advance in knowledge..." Martin Luther, *Sermons on Gospel Texts for Pentecost*, vol. 2, pt. 1, *The Complete Sermons of Martin Luther*, ed. John Nicholas Lenker, trans. Lenker et al. (Minneapolis: Lutherans in All Lands, 1907; reprint, Grand Rapids, MI: Baker Books, 2000), 409–10.

2 Yves Congar, "Pour Une Christologie Pneumatologique," *Revue des Sciences Philosophiques et Theologiques* 63 (1979): 435–42 [Eng., I Believe in the Holy Spirit, vol. 3, trans. David Smith (New York: Seabury, 1983; Reprint, New York: Crossroad, 1997), 165–73]. Jesus' giving of the Holy Spirit to others in baptism depends in a defining way on the Father's prior anointing of Jesus with the Spirit at the Jordan (see especially Lk 3:16, 21–22, and Acts 1:4–5, 2:33–39). Our resurrection by the Spirit of God also depends on the Father's raising of Jesus according to the Spirit of holiness (see Rom 1:3–4, 8:11, 22–23).

3 For a fuller study, see Leopoldo A. Sánchez M., "Receiver, Bearer, and Giver of God's Spirit: Jesus' Life and Mission in the Spirit as a Ground for Understanding Christology,

Trinity, and Proclamation" (Ph.D. diss., Concordia Seminary, St. Louis, 2003); "God against Us and for Us: Preaching Jesus in the Spirit," *Word & World* 24, no.2 (2003): 134–45; "La misión conjunta del Hijo y del Espíritu Santo en el misterio de Cristo: La vida y el ministerio de Jesús como receptor, portador y dador del Espíritu," in *Pneumatología: El Espíritu Santo y la espiritualidad de la iglesia* (St. Louis, Missouri: Editorial Concordia, 2005); "A Missionary Theology of the Holy Spirit: The Father's Anointing of Jesus and Its Implications for the Church in Mission," *Missio Apostolica* 14, no.1 (May 2006): 28–40.

4 See, for example, Raniero Cantalamesa, *The Holy Spirit in the Life of Jesus: The Mystery of Christ's Baptism*, trans. Alan Neame (Collegeville, MN.: The Liturgical Press, 1994).

5 The classic work is Virgilio Elizondo, *Galilean Journey: The Mexican-American Promise* (Maryknoll, NY: Orbis, 2000); see also his essays on "*Mestizaje* and a Galilean Christology," in *Beyond Borders: Writings of Virgilio Elizondo and Friends*, ed. Timothy Matovina (Maryknoll, NY: Orbis), 159–186.

6 See, for example, Segundo Galilea, *Teología de la Liberación: Ensayo de Síntesis*, Colección Iglesia Nueva (Bogotá, Colombia: Indo-American Press, 1978), 17.

7 In the most recent introduction to his classic work, Gustavo Gutiérrez offers a similar clarification on the non-exclusive sense of "preferential option for the poor." See *A Theology of Liberation: History, Politics, and Salvation*, ed. and trans. Sister Caridad Inda and John Eagleson, rev. ed. (Maryknoll, NY: Orbis, 1973; new introduction, 1988), xxv–xxviii.

8 Rubén Blades, "Blackamán," en *Agua de Luna*, CD 60721-2, Elektra, 1987.

9 "I need to know about seventeenth-century Puritans in order to make sense of the rebellion I notice everywhere in the American city. Teach me about mad British kings so I will understand the American penchant for iconoclasm. Then teach me about cowboys and Indians; I should know that tragedies created the country that will create me. Once you toss out Benjamin Franklin and Andrew Jackson, you toss out Navajos. You toss out immigrant women who worked the sweatshops of the Lower East Side. Once you toss out Thomas Jefferson, you toss out black history." Richard Rodriguez, *Days of Obligation: An Argument with My Mexican Father* (New York: Viking, 1992), 169–70.

10 Daisy L. Machado, "Kingdom Building in the Borderlands: The Church and Manifest Destiny," in *Hispanic/Latino Theology: Challenge and Promise*, ed. Ada María Isasi-Díaz and Fernando F. Segovia (Minneapolis: Fortress, 1996). The First Hispanic National Convention of the LCMS, under the leadership of its first president, Rev. Eloy González, expressed often this historic and bittersweet ambiguity of being a Hispanic Christian. In the preface to the Convention essays, I observed: "Our inherited paradox tells us that the cross, although a symbol often used to legimitize oppression and indifference toward the sufferer, remains ultimately in Christ crucified and risen, a true source of faith, hope, and love in the midst of poverty, abuse, marginalization, and even death." *Under the Cross of Christ—Yesterday, Today, and Forever: Reflections on Lutheran Hispanic Ministry in the United States* (St. Louis: Concordia Seminary Press, 2004).

11 For an edition of the classic with Kaufmann's 1970 translation, see Martin Buber, *I and Thou*, trans. Martin Kaufmann (New York: Touchstone, 1996).

12 John Zizioulas, *Being as Communion: Studies in Personhood and the Church* (Crestwood, NY: St. Vladimir's Seminary, 1985).

13 Jürgen Moltmann, *The Trinity and the Kingdom: The Doctrine of God* (Minneapolis: Fortress, 1993); Leonardo Boff, *Trinity and Society*, trans. Paul Burns, Theology and Liberation Series (Maryknoll, NY: Orbis, 1988); Catherine Mowry LaCugna, *God for Us: The Trinity and Christian Life* (New York: HarperCollins, 1991).

14 "Among us the question is not, as it keeps being described in Europe, how to do theology *after Auschwitz*, but doing it *in Auschwitz*, that is, in the midst of a terrifying cross..." Jon Sobrino, *Jesus the Liberator: A Historical-Theological View* (Maryknoll, NY: Orbis, 1993), 195.

[15] In response to Thomas Aquinas, Jesuit theologian John J. O'Donnell offers some limitations of classical theism for thinking of God in relation to time and history. *The Mystery of the Triune God* (New York: Paulist, 1989), 1–16. For a Lutheran response to classical and open theists, see Reed Lessing, "Pastor, Does God Really Respond to My Prayers?" *Concordia Journal* 32, no. 3 (2006): 256–273.

[16] Samuel Soliván, *The Spirit, Pathos and Liberation* (Sheffield, England: Sheffield, 1998).

[17] Martin Luther, "The Freedom of the Christian," in *Martin Luther's Basic Theological Writings*, ed. Timothy Lull (Minneapolis: Fortress, 1989), 596.

[18] "There are some who think that they have God and everything they need when they have money and property; they trust in them and boast in them so stubbornly and securely that they care for no one else. They, too, have a god—mammon by name, that is money and property—on which they set their whole heart. This is the most common idol on earth," Martin Luther, LC, "First Commandment," 5–6, in *The Book of Concord: The Confessions of the Evangelical Lutheran Church*, ed. Robert Kolb and Timothy J. Wengert (Minneapolis: Fortress, 2000), 387.

[19] Gustaf Wingren, *Luther on Vocation*, trans. Carl C. Rasmussen (reprint, Evansville, Indiana: Ballast Press, 1994); Paul Althaus, *The Ethics of Martin Luther*, trans. Robert C. Schultz (Philadelphia: Fortress, 1972); Robert Kolb, "Luther on the Two Kinds of Righteousness," *Lutheran Quarterly* 13, no. 4 (Winter 1999): 449–466; Charles P. Arand, "Two Kinds of Righteousness as a Framework for Law and Gospel in the Apology," *Lutheran Quarterly* 15, no. 4 (Winter 2001): 417–439; Joel Biermann, "Virtue Ethics and the Place of Character Formation within Lutheran Theology" (Ph.D. diss., Concordia Seminary, St. Louis, 2002).

[20] I want to thank my wife Tracy L. Sánchez and Center for Hispanic Studies guest instructor Deaconess Rose L. Gilbert for engaging me in conversation on this topic and helping me formulate my thoughts in parts of this section of the essay.

[21] Particularly helpful in this dimension of Christ's life in the Spirit is Cantalamesa's last chapter in *The Holy Spirit in the Life of Jesus*. See fn. 6.

[22] For a fuller study of prayer as a central expression of sonship, see Leopoldo A. Sánchez M., "Praying to God the Father in the Spirit: Reclaiming the Church's Participation in the Son's Prayer Life," *Concordia Journal* 32, no. 3 (2006): 274–295.

[23] Cited in Paul Althaus, *The Ethics of Martin Luther* (Minneapolis: Fortress, 1972), 104. Althaus explains further: "We can worship God by resting; indeed, in resting we can worship him better than in any other way because it is when we really relax our body and soul that we cast our care on God. We thus honor God as the one whose blessing rests upon and surrounds all our work, and who keeps on working for us even when we rest and sleep. The capacity truly to rest from our cares with our body and soul is a special confirmation of our faith and is related to justifying faith. The high value which Luther puts on resting protects him from any idolization of work" (Ibid.).

Religion and Religiosity

Paul W. Robinson

Pluralism and Mix-and-Match Religion

National Public Radio ran the following story on its "Morning Edition" program on January 12, 2007.

> If Gillian Siple had to describe herself in one word, it would be "spiritual." A senior at Davidson College in North Carolina, Siple spent the past year traveling and studying in Asia and Europe, immersing herself in religions other than her own.
>
> Amid an abundance of information about religion easily available via the Internet and television, she says, "Maybe the youth of today aren't sure if the way of their parents is perhaps the way that they want to follow, and I think that's wonderful."
>
> With a small group of students, Siple, a religion major, lived in China, Thailand and India. She meditated in monasteries and ashrams, lived and studied among Buddhists, Muslims, Hindus—not your typical study-abroad program.
>
> She remembers living at a meditation center in Thailand, wearing the traditional garb of a yogi. "I remember waking up at 4 o'clock in the morning and taking out my mat and I can remember just thinking, 'What if my friends saw me now? Would anyone recognize me? I am so far from the person and the life that I live back at Davidson right now. There's no remnant of that life on my body right now.'"

> Even her faith began to fall away. She says that when she meditated, she felt an uncommon sense of peace. She wondered: Have I gone into this too deeply? Am I still a Christian, or am I becoming something else?
>
> But back at Davidson College, she returned to the faith she knows best: Christianity. That faith is stronger now, she says. She attends prayer and fellowship meetings and heads an interfaith group on campus. She also meditates based on the teaching she learned in Thailand.
>
> Siple calls herself a Christian pluralist, open to the possibility of the validity of other religious traditions.
>
> After her tour of Asia, she spent a week at the Taize monastery in France, a place that attracts young people from around the world. In a Taize service, there is chanting and reading from scripture. But there are also long moments where more than 1,000 young adults sit quietly together in silence—not being told what to do.
>
> "You do what you feel is right for your religious practice," Siple says. "I think that is what our generation is screaming for right now. People want not to be told what they should do, but to figure it out for themselves."

How many women and men like Gillian are members of Lutheran congregations? It would be very difficult to say, and good Lutherans may not always act on their impulses to mix and match. Nevertheless, the assumptions, attitudes, and understandings that lead to the practice of mix-and-match religion surround us. They are embedded in the media, in our educational system, in our neighborhoods, and in our workplaces. This essay will briefly document how we got here and then offer some possible directions for our witness.

Pluralism in America

The phenomenon of mix-and-match religion can trace its origins to religious pluralism in America. Religious pluralism is, in one sense, rooted in the founding documents of the United States. Arguments concerning the establishment of religion in the newly independent colonies led eventually to the statement in the First Amendment that "Congress shall make no law respecting an establishment of religion, or prohibiting the free exercise thereof." Although some states took several decades to comply with disestablishment and many more maintained religious tests for office-holders in their constitutions well into the nineteenth century, America was determined to distinguish itself from Europe in how it considered relations between church and state. Even though the resulting American pluralism was initially overwhelmingly Christian and particularly Protestant, pluralism was the ideal, since it was concomitant with the removal of the church from affairs of state.

Such pluralism, it can be effectively argued, is essential for the equitable functioning of a democratic system of government. According to William Connolly, a pluralism of the public square responds to political necessity:

> A basic challenge of ethico-political life in late modern territorial states is how to negotiate honorable public settlements in settings where interdependent partisans confess different existential faiths and final sources of morality.[1]

The answer to this challenge, Connolly says, is pluralism with a bicameral edge or orientation. He describes the person with a bicameral orientation as one who keeps "a foot in two worlds, straddling two or more perspectives to maintain tension between them." The first perspective is the faith itself; the second perspective is "the engrained sense that you should exercise presumptive receptivity toward others when drawing that faith, creed, or philosophy into the public realm." What that means is "you love your creed; you seldom leave it entirely in the closet when you enter politics. But you appreciate how it appears opaque and profoundly contestable to many who do not participate in it; and you struggle against the tendency to resent this very state of affairs."[2] Connolly does not suggest that faith must change as a result of encounters in the public square. He does, however, consider it absolutely essential for believers to understand the points at which others do not share their faith and to overcome resentment of this state of affairs. Additionally, pluralism with a bicameral orientation requires believers to value tolerance above almost anything else in order to avoid multiplying actions or attitudes that might be considered intolerable provocation over matters of faith.

A pluralism of the public square can certainly lean in the direction of thinking that all religions are more or less the same, but that belief is not required for the type of pluralism endorsed by Connolly. Pluralism of the public square merely recognizes and lives with the reality that Americans hold to a bewildering variety of religious and spiritual beliefs. One can be a pluralist in this sense without also believing that all religions are more or less the same. Yet precisely this sort of agnostic pluralism—believing that ultimate religious truth cannot be known and, therefore, all religions are equivalent—has become prevalent in America. The agnostic pluralism we see all around us today developed out of the widespread questioning of Christianity's truth claims rooted in the ideas and attitudes of the Enlightenment.

The Enlightenment view of religion is typified in Gotthold Ephraim Lessing's play *Nathan the Wise*. Set during the Third Crusade, the play is a dialogue about religion between Nathan, who is a Jewish merchant, the Sultan Saladin, and a Templar Knight. The centerpiece of the story is a parable about a magical ring passed down from father to son. The ring had the power to make its wearer pleasing in the eyes of both God and people. One wearer of the ring had three sons. Rather than decide which of them should receive the ring, he promised it to all three and had two copies of the ring made. It was impossible to tell who had the genuine ring, and the sons began to quarrel. A judge admonished each to live as if he wore the genuine ring. So in the same way, the Jew, the Muslim, and the Christian were to live as if their religion were the one, true religion. The implication, of course, is that the ethical dimension of religious life is of supreme importance and belief matters only insofar as it leads to right conduct.

Enlightenment ideas easily penetrated the American context and, for example, animated Thomas Jefferson's approach to Christianity. Jefferson's *The Life and Morals of Jesus of Nazareth Selected Textually from the Gospels*, also called the Jefferson Bible, is a compilation of biblical passages that define and describe the ethical system of Jesus. For Jefferson, this work represented genuine Christianity as lessons in how to live like Jesus rather than beliefs about his person. Reductionist understandings of Christianity have always been quite common on the American scene, and a preoccupation with ethical conduct similar to Jefferson's frequently drives popular reaction to pluralist ideas. If one observes that good people can be Jewish, Catholic, Presbyterian, Buddhist, or Muslim, then one concludes that these religious traditions are equally valuable and valid, and that view is supported with pluralist ideology.

Enlightenment thinking took root in America and provided the foundation for a certain type of pluralism—a pluralism that tends to devalue the truth claims of all religions by assuming they are equivalent or reducing them to systems of morality. As a popular phenomenon in America, pluralism of this sort was strengthened by the first Parliament of World Religions held in Chicago in 1893. Although the majority of those who attended the parliament were Christians, the gathering was intended to honor all the great world religions. The Parliament was promoted as a great achievement of American culture, but, as the Archbishop of Canterbury pointed out, that achievement was to consider all the major religions functionally equivalent. This agnostic attitude toward the ultimate truth of various religions has come to characterize American religious pluralism.

Deep religious pluralism is pluralism of yet another type. For example, John Cobb—the twentieth-century process theologian whose name has become synonymous with Christocentric pluralism—begins from a philosophical assumption rather than a practical challenge as does most agnostic pluralism. In other words, deep religious pluralists do not assume that they cannot know whether a religion is true. Rather, Cobb, for example, assumes that "every great tradition is based on some deep insight into, some revelation about—whichever language one prefers—the nature of things."[3] He both rejects the a priori denial of any other authentic religion than Christianity and, unlike some other pluralist thinkers, affirms that there are in fact other such religions. Cobb builds his system on the thought of Alfred North Whitehead. Whitehead called Buddhism and Christianity the "two great Catholic traditions." He then added science to them as a third, in that he believed theology and science had to be modified each in light of the other. Although Whitehead himself rejected many claims of modern science as untenable, he held that its fundamental naturalism was an inescapable truth and dictated how religion could describe the relationship between God and the world. So, too, for Cobb "the universal truth offered by modern science" is essential to the pluralist enterprise.[4] Cobb encourages a continual encounter between science, Christianity, and other faiths as the only way to make Christianity a truly global religion. For him, such encounters lead not to relativism but to a genuine transformation of Christianity that is rooted in devotion to the living Christ rather than to specific forms of the faith.

Deep religious pluralism, represented by Cobb, and pluralism with a bicameral orientation, represented by Connolly, have both benefited from modernity, that is, from the Enlightenment tradition in American thought. Connolly, for example, writes from a consciously modern perspective, addressing the problems of the late modern nation-state and defending his proposals against charges of postmodern "relativism" and "rootlessness." John Cobb, too, takes pains to defend the contributions of the Enlightenment and, as we have seen, builds on Whitehead's positioning of science as one of the great traditions. The privileging of science distinguishes these pluralist approaches as fundamentally modern, rather than postmodern, and positions them to take advantage of the pragmatic and practical orientation of much of American society. Pluralism represents, in a very real way, the final triumph of Enlightenment thinking about religion.

Mix-and-Match Religion

The next step from the popular pluralism just described is to appropriate beliefs and practices from a variety of religious and philosophical systems. As long as American society agreed on a Judeo-Christian ethic and while denominational affiliation was an important part of church life, individuals showed little tendency toward mix-and-match spirituality. But individualism, always a tendency in the culture, has finally and profoundly changed the American religious orientation. Robert Bellah famously described the trend in his book *Habits of the Heart*:

> Sheila Larson is a young nurse who has received a good deal of therapy and describes her faith as "Sheilaism." This suggests the logical possibility of more than 235 million American religions, one for each of us. "I believe in God," Sheila says. "I am not a religious fanatic. [Notice at once that in our culture any strong statement of belief seems to imply fanaticism so you have to offset that.] I can't remember the last time I went to church. My faith has carried me a long way. It's Sheilaism. Just my own little voice." Sheila's faith has some tenets beyond belief in God, though not many. In defining what she calls "my own Sheilaism," she said: "It's just try to love yourself and be gentle with yourself. You know, I guess, take care of each other. I think God would want us to take care of each other." Like many others, Sheila would be willing to endorse few more specific points.[5]

What Bellah and others decried as individualist destruction of communal faith has more recently been described neutrally as a shift in the religious landscape.[6] The individual approach to religion means that the only logic pertaining to religious belief as a system is that of the individual. Whether or not an individual's religion becomes as reductionist as Sheilaism, individual choice trumps any judgment regarding the logical coherence of belief.

Mix-and-match religion can lead to some interesting combinations, to say the least. One of these, the combination of Judaism and Buddhism, has even acquired a descriptive label: JuBu. Although the popularity of this particular combination can be traced to the fascination with all things Zen prevalent in the 1960s (Alan Ginsburg was a prominent JuBu), its origin can be found in the penetration of eastern religious ideas into America beginning in the late nineteenth century. This example merely highlights how prevalent mix-and-match attitudes are and demonstrates how problematic American "spirituality" has become.

According to recent research by the Barna Institute, 62% of Americans consider themselves to be "deeply spiritual." This does not, however, correlate to specific moral standards or even to the belief that there is absolute moral truth.

> The research confirmed that the younger a person is, the less likely they are to trust the Bible as their source of moral guidance or to believe that absolute moral truth exists. For instance, 20% of adults 60 or older base their moral choices on the Bible and 18% of Baby Boomers do so, but only 13% of Baby Busters and a mere 9% of Mosaics follow suit. In the same manner, while four out of ten Boomers and Builders say moral truth is absolute, just 32% of Busters and 25% of Mosaics hold that view.[7]

The results suggest that for younger Americans no strong link between belief and morality exists. This is not simply a matter of people failing to live up to the beliefs they profess or failing to make logical connections between life and belief. Religious belief no longer guarantees a moral absolute, and logic is no longer valued in connecting belief and life, or even in connecting varying beliefs. The trend represents, perhaps, a final unraveling of religious belief from traditional church life; it expresses the fact that many who consider themselves spiritual are living in a faith community of one.

Mix-and-match religion as the individual's approach to constructing belief is aided and abetted by postmodernism. In contrast to pluralism more narrowly considered, mix-and-match religion is opposed to the general direction and tenets of modernism. An approach to religion that demonstrates "an incredulity toward metanarratives," to use Lyotard's definition of postmodernism, cannot privilege any particular religious discourse, even that of science.[8] From the mix-and-match standpoint, all systems are equally capable of truth. This is a different stance from both deep religious and agnostic pluralism. Deep religious pluralists do make judgments about the value of various religious claims. For agnostic pluralists the value of different religious truth claims is by definition indeterminable. But in mix-and-match religion meaning is created by an individual's choice and value is determined by how well a truth claim "works." An individual's choice of a particular belief or practice creates meaning without denying the possibility of meaning and capacity for truth of practices and beliefs that he or she personally does not hold.

This potential equality of belief is, of course, only true theoretically. In practice, individual choice in the midst of a bewildering array of religious systems results in a de facto canon of values. In other words, some attitudes and beliefs are more equal than others. A striking example comes from a report on the revival of ancient Greek religion. A small group gathered near the ruins of a temple on the Acropolis in Athens to honor Zeus. The date was January 21, 2007. The twenty pagans involved in the ceremony represented a campaign to restore the religion of ancient

Greece. Yet the values the worshipers brought to the ritual seem anything but ancient.

> "Our message is world peace and an ecological way of life in which everyone has the right to education," said Kostas Stathopoulos, one of three high priests overseeing the event, which celebrated the nuptials of Zeus and Hera, the goddess of love and marriage.[9]

The report never mentioned blood sacrifice or the fear that the gods should command. A return to the old ways can be justified, apparently, only if it conforms to present-day values of ecology and education. Incredulity regarding metanarratives only goes so far when mixing and matching religions.

Conclusion

Pastors and congregations have a difficult task as they reach out to communities saturated with the ideas and assumptions inherent in pluralism and mix-and-match religion. How do you make the case for Christ among people who assume that one religion is pretty much like every other religion? How do you dialogue with people who respect your Christian faith, and even claim to be Christians themselves, but also incorporate other, contradictory beliefs, such as reincarnation, into their worldviews?

The situation is difficult and complex not only outside our congregations but within them as well. Americans in general are less biblically literate and less loyal to a specific denomination than ever before. Some of this is a result of the predominance of mainline, liberal Protestantism. Many denominations do not have the same commitment to unity in faith that they once had. But similar phenomena can be observed even among conservative Lutherans. This is not so much a failure of catechetical effort as it is a need to refocus our catechesis, especially once we have recognized that the Christian faith no longer enjoys the broad cultural support that it once had in America.

When faced with a complex situation, we are tempted to respond with a complex solution or set of solutions. But to answer every objection raised by pluralists and to respond to every whim of the mix-and-match religionist is not only impossible but counterproductive. The response to our cultural situation that will best serve Lutheranism in the long run is to focus our attention, effort, and energy on our central message—the core belief in forgiveness of sins by grace, through faith, because of Christ.

Let us consider two examples of how congregational efforts might be focused more precisely on the forgiveness of sins. The first is making our congregations places where forgiveness is practiced. The trend among churches today, especially in the emerging church movement, is to talk about authenticity. For most people that means living in a way that lines up with your beliefs and matching your actions to your words. In many ways, this is precisely what Lutheran thinking on vocation and the priesthood of the baptized has always meant. Many congregations respond to cries for authenticity by organizing myriad service projects and volunteer mission trips. Without denigrating those activities in the least, I would suggest that genuinely Lutheran "authenticity" needs to go deeper. If our core belief is forgiveness of sins, that is what people both outside and inside need to see in our congregations. David Hilton observes that all too often Christian congregations do not look like places that people in need of forgiveness would gather.

> We all get dressed up on Sunday, and we go [to church] and say, Isn't it great, all these good people! So I don't dare share my pain and brokenness with you because you might reject me. We sit there with our pain and our brokenness, and we never share it and we don't heal. Our church's real challenge in the next decade or two is to find out how we can change from being congregations of pretense to being healing communities; we have to work toward becoming the kind of communities where it's safe to tell your life story.[10]

Congregations like this will make sense to those looking for authenticity. That in itself is not, of course, sufficient reason. Congregations like this are also genuinely Lutheran.

The second example of focusing on forgiveness is how pastors and congregations might focus their efforts in catechesis. Traditional catechesis has tended to focus on answering the objections posed to Lutheranism by modernity. The classic example is the need to defend creation against the beliefs and assumptions of evolution. The problem with this approach is that in the current situation we are no longer faced with a single, dominant worldview. There may be as many different worldviews, with different attendant questions and objections, as there are people in the new-members class. Openness to questions being asked by the culture is still critical. Just recognize that there are far more and very different questions than there were before. Even though American society as a whole exhibits certain attitudes and behaviors, individuals have, in many cases, formed their own system of beliefs and values. There is, therefore, no single, appropriate method or approach to teaching the faith. More than ever before, instruction must be tailored to specific situations and even specific individuals.

That is not to say that catechesis should begin by responding to every question and objection of those coming to Christianity from some other belief system. In fact, I believe the opposite is true. When we present the faith, we are telling our story. We are sharing what we believe—indeed, what we know to be true—about Jesus and the love God has for fallen human beings. So teaching the faith need not proceed based on propositional truth and intellectual assent to first principles. Rather it can focus on the great story of how God forgives (remember the Lutheran core value!) as shown in stories—Old Testament and New Testament stories, your story, and my story. After all, is it more important when teaching the faith to have those we are teaching able to answer any possible objection or to have them believe, fervently and firmly, that they are God's forgiven people in Christ?

Endnotes

1 William E. Connolly, *Pluralism* (Durham: Duke University Press, 2005), 34.
2 Ibid., 4.
3 David Ray Griffin, "John Cobb's Whiteheadian Complementary Religious Pluralism" in *Deep Religious Pluralism*, (Louisville, KY: Westminster John Knox Press, 2005), 44.
4 Ibid., 44.
5 Robert N. Bellah, et al. *Habits of the Heart: Individualism and Commitment in American Life*, updated edition with a new introduction. (Berkeley: University of California Press, 1996), 221.
6 Martin Marty, "Revising the Map of American Religion" *Annals of the American Academy of Political and Social Science* 558:13–27.
7 "Most Adults Feel Accepted by God, but Lack a Biblical Worldview," The Barna Update (August 9, 2005).
8 Jean-François Lyotard, *The Postmodern Condition: A Report on Knowledge* (Manchester: Manchester University Press, 1984), xxiv.
9 Paris Ayiomamitis, "Ceremony in Athens seeks to revive ancient pagan religion," The Associated Press, *St. Louis Post-Dispatch*, 22 January 2007.
10 David Hilton, "Global health and the limits of medicine: an interview with Dave Hilton." *Second Opinion* 18:3, January 1993.

David R. Schmitt

American Mystic Spirituality

Richard Lischer's first call was to an LCMS congregation in rural Illinois. There, he struggled in spiritual growth, a struggle he has recorded in his memoir, *Open Secrets*. In one story, Lischer relates how God integrates an outsider into the congregation. Lischer first glimpsed Teri from the pulpit, a mysterious presence in the back pew who "invariably arrived late and left before anyone could greet her."[1] Later, he had his first conversation with her. It was by flashlight, in a darkened church, in the middle of the night. She had been "breaking into the church—to pray." As a pastor, he tried to explain to her that this "could be your church." Unsuccessful in that approach, he found that all he could do was offer her a key: "Over the next few months, she would continue to break into the church to pray, usually on Saturday nights, and I would continue to offer her a key."[2] Faced with a mysterious woman, separated from the church and yet drawn to it in private spiritual practice, Lischer learned to practice the art of hospitality before engaging in explanation.

While Teri's subsequent story would not place her among American mystics, Lischer's image of her can introduce our contemplation of mystic spirituality and the mind of Christ. American mystic spirituality is a mysterious presence, often lingering on the outskirts of the Lutheran congregation. Separated from the institutional church and yet drawn to it for private spiritual practice, American mystics seem prone to breaking in rather than entering by baptism or the front door. Pastors who attend to the mystics in American culture could learn from Lischer. American mystic spirituality is best engaged by practices of hospitality before explanation. The following essay seeks to foster such hospitality; it examines the character of American mystic spirituality through the pages of spiritual autobiography,[3] so that in time one might begin a conversation with these guests.

Mysticism notoriously defies definition.[4] For the sake of clarity, in this essay, American mystic spirituality is understood to be the beliefs and practices that surround an individual's desire for an immediate experience of God, an experience that remains outside of institutional and personal control and that, when encountered, fosters a vibrant spiritual life appreciative of mystery.

American Mystic Spirituality and the Local Congregation

At the heart of American mystic spirituality lies a paradoxical relationship with the church. God is experienced within the forms of the institutional church and yet remains outside of ecclesial control, and sometimes even outside of ecclesial awareness. The local congregation is frequently an unknowing host of the holy. Annie Dillard, perhaps the most celebrated female American mystic, records her surprise at an encounter with the holy in a Presbyterian congregation of her youth. For Dillard, the adults of Shadyside Presbyterian in Pittsburgh were blind to the power of the Word. They sent their children to Bible camp, had them dutifully memorize Bible verses, and yet "didn't recognize the vivid danger that we would, through repeated exposure, catch a case of its wild opposition to their world."[5] Sitting in the balcony one Sunday morning, Dillard rebels. She takes a prolonged look at the congregation, "the putative hypocrisy of the expensive men and women," and knows "what the barefoot Christ, if there had been such a person, would think about things—grape juice, tailcoats, British vowels, sable stoles." Dillard "knew enough of the Bible to damn these people to hell, citing chapter and verse."[6]

Yet, in the midst of her prolonged look at the human, she catches a momentary glimpse of the divine: "I was alert enough now to feel, despite myself, some faint, thin stream of spirit braiding forward from the pews. Its flawed and fragile rivulets pooled far beyond me at the altar" and ultimately gathered together "in the gold mosaic's dome." There, the gold mosaic of Christ, barefoot and floating, "scattered some spirit, like light back over the cavernous room, and held some of it, like light, in its deep curve."[7] As Dillard experiences the silence of congregational prayer and the voice of Scriptural memory, she stands isolated from prayer and from the people whom she condemns. Yet, in the face of human silence and an alienating Scriptural voice, Dillard has a mystical experience, somehow centered in Christ, wherein "there was no speech nor language" and she "didn't know what to make of it."[8] Through this experience, Dillard ironically becomes an unwilling member of this congregation, a part of this community at prayer that serves as an unknowing host to the holy breaking into the world.

In terms of American mystical autobiography, Dillard's experience is typical in three ways. First, her desire for God leads her into the physical sites and spiritual practices of the Christian community. American mystics, both those who have had such experiences and those who desire them, chronicle how they hover around churches, sites of the holy, awaiting an experience of the divine. In *Stalking the Divine*, skeptical freelance journalist Kristin Ohlson is searching for "after-Christmas sales" when she humorously stumbles upon a newspaper ad for Christmas services at the St. Paul shrine in Cleveland.[9] Her ambivalent attendance at this service ("even if I didn't share their convictions, I thought it possible to be infected by their fervor, to pick up a tiny germ of faith that might quicken and grow"[10]) ultimately leads her to interview the Poor Clares of Perpetual Adoration who attend service with her but worship behind a screen. For Ohlson, the mystical experience of God was certainly occurring in the nuns' enclosure, just as it had occasionally occurred to her as a child. She finds herself now torn by longing: longing to recover that "stunned ecstasy" of childhood,[11] longing to uncover the spirituality of the Poor Clares, and longing to discover all of this in the practices of worship. Yet, repeatedly, Ohlson finds herself worshipping in a congregational space, bound by screens, where the mystery of the holy remains always beyond her reach.

Second, Dillard's stance in relationship to that community of faith is deeply conflicted. Dillard finds herself distanced from the worship service, observing the practices of others rather than engaging in them herself. In a similar way, Ohlson finds herself returning to the Catholicism of her childhood, something she had previously put away. Paradoxically, the desire for an immediate experience of God draws American mystics to the physical sites and spiritual practices of ecclesial communities that they have already rejected as intermediaries. One thinks of Thomas Merton. In his spiritual autobiography, Merton symbolically figures himself as the child of a church in ruins. He remembers his childhood fascination with pictures of ancient cathedrals and monasteries, and his intimations of the holy when he physically sat in the shadows of ancient ruins.[12] The ecclesial ruins physically encountered in childhood are spiritually denounced in adulthood as Merton rejects the Christian church.[13] Fueled by the study of Blake and an interest in mysticism, Merton engages in a spiritual search that leads him away from the church to Bramachari, a monastic follower of the Hindu Messiah, Jagad-Bondhu. Merton's rejection of Christianity, however, does not lead to God working immediately in another religious context to bring Merton to faith. Instead, God ironically works through Bramachari, a Hindu monk, to direct Merton back to the Christian tradition he had earlier rejected.[14] There, within the ruins of the Christian church, Merton will experience the divine revelations he so greatly desires.

Prompted by an inner voice, Merton enters "the little brick Church of Corpus Christi, hidden behind Teachers College on 121st Street."[15] Here, in the proclamation of the Word, Merton, "a blind and deaf and dumb pagan as weak and dirty as anything that ever came out of the darkness of Imperial Rome or Corinth or Ephesus," experiences a transformation beyond his understanding so that "all I did know is that I walked in a new world."[16] Merton's trope of paganism highlights his sense of transgression. Already upon entering the church, Merton feared that "people had spotted me for a pagan and were just waiting for me to miss a few more genuflections before throwing me out."[17] He recognizes that he does not belong and flees in fear at the consecration of the elements.[18] He even ponders what it would have been like if in the past he had "discovered the Divinity of Christ in the ancient mosaics of the churches of Rome."[19] Yet God comes to Merton not in the ruins of the churches of the past but in the ruins of the present. As Merton breaks into the spiritual practices of the church he had rejected, God breaks into Merton's world. Repeated divine revelations slowly lead Merton into deeper inexplicable experiences of faith and community, fostering and forming his vocation as a monk. It should not surprise the reader that Merton, who earlier had gazed upon pictures of churches and monasteries, should discover his vocation when gazing upon "a great big picture of the hermitages of the Camaldolese."[20] Here, with echoes of Augustine[21] and Teresa,[22] Merton experiences something akin to rapture: these images "pierced me to the heart like a knife" and he "went out of the library, trying to stamp out the embers that had broken into flame, there, for an instant, within me."[23]

Third, Dillard's experience of the divine in a church she has rejected is cloaked in double-edged irony. As already noted, the American mystic reluctantly comes to the local congregation, assuming it to be devoid of the divine, only to discover life. This divine experience stands in contrast not only to the mystic's expectations but also to the expectations of those within the congregation. In American mystical spiritual autobiographies, those who gather around the things of God are often ironically unaware of the divine presence at work in their midst. It is the outsider, who begrudgingly stands within the ecclesial community, who receives a divine revelation of the depth of God's working that goes beyond what the members of the community believe. In these accounts, the church often stands as a careless steward of God's sacred mysteries.

Writer Reynolds Price reflected on his experience in this way:

> the few times I've gone to church in recent years, I'm immediately asked if I'll coach the Little League team or give a talk on Wednesday night or come to the men's bell-ringing class on Sunday afternoon. Church has become a full-service entertainment facility. It ought to be the place where God lives.[24]

For Price, this struggle is not new. Even as a child, he sought to integrate his mystical experiences into the life offered within the confines of the institutional church. The answer for him was a spiritual life of withdrawal from the church that paradoxically brought him closer to God: "The further I moved from organized worship, the more the God of my childhood meant to me—and the Christ that I thought I discerned in the warring pictures of the gospels."[25] As he notes, his withdrawal was not alone. Price takes with him the word that God has given the church.

While his visions of God and divine locutions are immediate, Price often recalls them within the context of God's word, the "warring pictures of the gospels" and the radical God one meets there.[26] As Price later notes, when he reflects on his vision of Jesus baptizing him in the Sea of Galilee, he is formed "by the texts and rites of an unchurchly Christianity."[27] In his phrase—"unchurchly Christianity"—Price captures the paradox of a community of faith fallen from the faith. He also reveals the common experience of mystics: the divine continues to work in ways beyond the recognition of those who consider themselves faithful. For Price, as for many American mystics, individual contemplation of God's word separates that word, through which and around which the Spirit gathers God's people, from community and, ultimately, sets that word against the very community that God gathers around it. At the heart of Price's mysticism lies the power of words, reflected in both his creative contemplation of Scripture and his written exploration of spiritual experiences.[28] When Price does return to visit churches, therefore, he does so as an outsider, coming "for lone worship," coming with a certainty of the power of the word, coming with a desire to hear and to use "words to convey a wordless knowledge of the core of light."[29] Repeatedly, however, he is keenly disappointed in the people and the practices he meets.

In spiritual autobiographies, American mystics often lurk in the shadows of the church, reluctantly breaking into its spiritual practices and community, drawn by a desire for an immediate experience of God. Paradoxically, their desire for divine immediacy draws them to divine intermediaries, intermediaries they have already judged as failed or at least flawed. Ironically, these divine intermediaries play unknowing host to the holy so that, within the spiritual practices of these communities, the mystic experiences the holy, only to discover that the holy remains outside of ecclesial awareness. American mystic spirituality is, therefore, fraught not only with paradox and tension but also with surprise. Divine presence occurs in ironic opposition both to the individual's past experiences (which have led to rejection of the church) and to the awareness of the community of the faithful. The individual is surprised by God as God remains surprisingly at work in a rejected and often benighted church. Having examined the American mystic's relationship with the local congregation, consider now the mystic's orientation toward the life of faith.

American Mystic Spirituality and the Life of Faith

One would expect that American mystic spirituality would foster an isolating religious interiority, a life of faith that moves the individual away from activity in the world and into highly privatized spiritual practices that promise moments of intimacy with the divine. Surprisingly, this is not so. While the life of faith that follows mystical experiences is not uniform for American mystics, it does exhibit a reluctance to sacralize particular spiritual practices as a means of preparing for the divine and it manifests a vibrant engagement with the world.

Spiritual Practices

In terms of spiritual practices, traditional configurations of the practices associated with mysticism involve purgation, illumination, and (depending upon divine favor) contemplation. In American mystical experience, the idea of some practice of purgation is strangely absent from their work. In chronicling their paths to and from mystical experience, American mystics do not focus upon the necessity of preparing oneself through various physical and mental practices for meeting the divine. This absence of purgation may be due in part to a different understanding of sin. For the American mystic, sin is less a matter of activities that have been done or not done before God and more a state of being in the world, an experience of meaninglessness. When God has been removed (as much as possible) from public discourse and local congregations are voluntary communities of like-minded individuals rather than those called by God and set apart for his work in his world, individuals can suffer from a sense of meaninglessness in everyday life. Life lacks meaning because it is not consciously experienced in the presence of God. A mystical revelation of God's presence (rather than forgiveness), therefore, brings an awareness of meaning. Life may not necessarily be changed but it is invested with meaning, because it is noticed and claimed by God.

For example, consider the spiritual dynamics of Price's mystical baptism in the Sea of Galilee. While baptism for Christians would evoke some association with the forgiveness of sin, for Price it was different. At the time, Price was suffering from a tumor growing in the nerve tissue located in his spine. In surgery, the doctors had removed only ten percent of the tumor and carved out some space in seven vertebrae of his upper spine both to accommodate any future growth of the tumor and to forestall the compression that would ultimately occur. At home, Price recovered from surgery and yet slowly became aware of progressive paralysis, a symptom of his cancerous approach toward death. On the morning of July 3, 1984, he found himself transported to the Sea of Galilee in a mystical vision. There, Jesus approached him, led him naked into the water, and baptized him, saying, "Your sins are forgiven," before turning to go back to the shore. Price's response was *"It's not my sins I'm worried about,"* (emphasis added) and he asked the receding Jesus, "Am I also cured?"[30] Price seeks information about his present experience while eternity hangs in the balance. Price is aware of the self-interested nature of his response, but he wants to communicate to the reader the primary value of this mystical experience. Price's mystical baptism is more important because of the meaning of God's presence in the present moment than because of any discussion of the forgiveness of sins and eternity.

As Price contemplates this vision, comfort is never taken in the forgiveness of sins. Rather, Price finds comfort in the way his vision confirmed two convictions: first, the belief that Jesus "bore a mysterious relation to the creator" and, second, the belief that "the creator takes close note of some creatures and apparently very little of others—a notice that's hardly egalitarian and that hardly always proves fortunate for the chosen creature or tribe."[31] Here, Price does not equate being noticed by God with prosperity in this life. In fact, he recognizes that "the creator's *chosen* die so often in torment."[32] Instead, being noticed by God gives Price's life meaning in the midst of suffering. Physical suffering and a debilitating descent into death have raised questions, questions not of sin and future judgment but of the ability of life, shortened and suffering, to have meaning. The mystical presence of God in the present moment gives that life meaning, regardless of what that life might be.

Later, Price receives communion from a Methodist minister. He notes, "I'd been raised in the Methodist church myself; and while I'd stopped attending years back, I kept a strong respect for the primary sacrament—communion."[33] As Price contemplates the sacrament, however, one again he notes that his focus is not on forgiveness but on the mystical sense of a presence, the presence of God that gives life meaning:

> Perhaps as intensely as any mystic, in the slow eating that one morning, I experienced again the almost overwhelming force which has always felt to me like God's presence. Whether the force would confirm my healing or go on

> devastating me, for the moment I barely cared. No prior taste in my old life had meant as much as this new chance at a washed and clarified view of my fate.[34]
>
> Here, God is valued not so much for what he does in Price's life (Price is willing to receive healing or continued suffering from God) but for the wonder that he does something. God's presence gives human life a meaning beyond human making. Price now has "a washed and clarified view" of life. When Price refers to his future with the impersonal language of "fate," he is not denying the existence of God (God's existence, after all, is what his confession affirms). Instead, he is communicating to the reader how he values God: God is not valued for what he might do for Price in the future; God is valued for the fact that he is with him in the present. When the future comes, whatever that "fate" may be, his "fate" has meaning because it comes to one who lives in the presence of God. Price celebrates his mystical experiences not because they bring assurance of the forgiveness of sins ("It's not my sins I'm worried about") but because they awaken him to the presence of God. Such a response is typical for these American mystics.

In an American culture that fosters a struggle for meaning, the American mystic celebrates glimpses of the unexplainable presence of God because that presence alone graces life with meaning. Thus, Merton configures his spiritual journey as that of the typical American hero.[35] Intoxicated with the freedom of self-creation, Merton engages in a quest for self-fulfillment. He becomes an American consumer, taking all that he can of life only to find that such taking paradoxically divests life of meaning:

> Here I was, scarcely four years after I had left Oakham and walked out into the world that I thought I was going to ransack and rob of all its pleasures and satisfactions. I had done what I intended, and now I found that it was I who was emptied and robbed and gutted. What a strange thing! In filling myself, I had emptied myself. In grasping things, I had lost everything. In devouring pleasures and joys, I had found distress and anguish and fear.[36]

Fulfilling the American dream, he discovers it to be a nightmare and awaits those moments of divine presence that will awaken him to life.

Dillard expands the focal field from American culture to the natural landscape. Yet, even here, she recognizes the threatening meaninglessness of life in light of the natural world. After a two-year stay in Roanoke Valley, Virginia, Dillard organizes her reflections in the Pulitzer Prize winning work, *Pilgrim at Tinker Creek*. She opens her reflections with what is either bestial or divine confrontation. Allah's question in the Koran captures the fight: "The heaven and the earth and all in between, thinkest thou I made them in jest?"[37] Throughout her journey, Dillard takes seriously the idea that life has no meaning, that it was created in jest; she carefully chronicles the workings of nature that would lead one to conclude that life is a joke. As she does so, however, she also captures those moments when an unbidden divine presence flashes forth, often in glimpses of beauty generated by acts of horrifying violence. This unexpected presence of the divine, beyond human understanding, enables her to hazard an answer at the end of her journey: "The universe was not made in jest but in solemn incomprehensible earnest. By a power that is unfathomably secret, and holy, and fleet. There is nothing to be done about it, but ignore it, or see."[38]

Yet, seeing the divine does not automatically flow from specified acts of purgation and holy preparation. In fact, to construct such a practice would be to attempt to impose meaning upon a meaningless life. These American mystics leave such meaning-making to God. Thus, while the meaninglessness of life may be one reason that American mystics forego spiritual practices of purgation, another reason may be the nature of the mystical experience of the divine. For these American mystics, you do not approach God as much as God approaches you and, with him, he brings the present moment filled by his presence with incomprehensible meaning. Thus, the meaningless world becomes filled with a meaning beyond your making, a meaning you will never comprehend, and that present world filled with meaning is being given to you by God.

Consider, for example, how Dillard imagines grace as an archer, piercing this world from and with eternity. Through this act of violence, the divine brings life.[39] Throughout her work, Dillard records moments of insight, times when she is lost in the wonderfully horrifying experience of the present moment: seeing the beauty of sharks suspended in water colored amber by the blood of their frenzied feeding; or capturing a glimpse of the "tree with the lights in it," where creation shines with an eternal light. Such moments are doors for Dillard. Yet, they are doors that do not open upon eternity, as if the mystic could somehow enter into the eternal presence of God through these moments. Rather, they are doors "opened *from* eternity," so that the mystic is brought into the present world where this world, this time, this space is filled with incomprehensible meaning by God. As Dillard writes, "That Christ's incarnation occurred improbably, ridiculously, at such-and-such a time, into such-and-such a place, is referred to—with great sincerity even among believers—as 'the scandal of particularity.' Well, the 'scandal of particularity' is the only world that I, in particular, know."[40] You do not leave this world to find God; God enters this world to find you and brings with him this world, the present moment, filled with a meaning beyond your making. One is awakened from the meaninglessness of life to find the exact same life, suddenly filled with meaning, because of the presence of God.

Such moments cannot be prepared for, or manufactured through spiritual practices and prayers. In her encounter with the Poor Clares of Perpetual Adoration, Ohlson makes this mistake. She anticipates that God will somehow come to her through an all-night vigil, her "first foray into extended prayer."[41] After her brief and painful adoption of the spiritual practices of the sisters, however, Ohlson discovers how difficult it is to prepare oneself for a revelation of God: "The all-night vigil seemed like a bit of a bust, at least as far as my own spiritual search was concerned ... I was a little disappointed that I hadn't been suffused with a sense of God's presence."[42] Price has a similar experience, after his baptismal vision at the Sea of Galilee. He notes how, at times, he would awaken to "the presence, just to the right in my mind's eye, of a patient listener behind a screen." This presence gave his present experience meaning: "Its reliable presence seemed only to say that I had somehow to build my life on radical uncertainty, knowing only that I was heard by something more than the loyal but powerless humans near me."[43] The radical certainty of divine presence gives Price the radical uncertainty of the present as a time within which to live. After his radiation ended, Price tried to duplicate these experiences but to no avail: "I've tried but have never had them again. No head and shoulders will pause to listen now; but it listened then."[44] Such experiences come from God at God's desire and thus are received by the mystic as a gift. Dillard plays upon this idea of receiving the present as a present from God as she writes,

> You do not run down the present, pursue it with baited hooks and nets. You wait for it, empty-handed, and you are filled. You'll have fish left over. The creek is the one great giver. It is, by definition, Christmas, the incarnation. This old rock planet gets the present for a present on its birthday every day.[45]

Engagement with the World

Because the divine has appeared to these individuals without preparation, a life of preparation for such an appearance is unnecessary. As one did nothing to create this experience, one cannot recreate it. Instead one finds that life is an attending to the experiences of this world with greater alertness, recognizing that anything can be a moment of the divine. This, then, is the remarkable vibrancy of the American mystic's life of faith: mystical experiences invite one to live in continual wonder, to approach all of life with reverence, since any moment has the potential suddenly to break into a revelation or radical presence of the divine. Mystical experiences, then, are not so much repositories of truths that enlighten individuals as they are invitations into lives of active contemplation, attending to a sense of mystery even as one attends to the ordinary activities of life in this world. For those unfamiliar with American mystic spirituality, the stunning nature of the revelations belies the effect of these experiences: rather than be drawn away from ordinary life into a world of fantastic raptures and visions, the mystic is thrust more fully into the everyday activities of this world, trusting that within such activities lies divine meaning, certainly beyond human understanding and frequently beyond human perception, but every once in a while experienced in a moment that draws one closer to the details of life in this world.

So, one finds Dillard awakened to the potential of every meaningless moment of life to have meaning, wandering in the natural world, recording her observations on note cards, and trusting in the divine presence that suddenly breaks forth. She writes,

> You can wait forgetful anywhere, for anywhere is the way of his fleet passage, and hope to catch him by the tail and shout something in his ear before he wrests away. Or you can pursue him wherever you dare, risking the shrunken sinew in the hollow of the thigh ... I sit on a bridge as on Pisgah or Sinai, and I am both waiting becalmed in a cliff of the rock and banging with all my will, calling like a child beating on a door: Come on out! ... I know you're there.[46]

All of life is a mystery for Dillard and all of life calls for a careful attending to, a waiting upon God or a stalking of the divine. Whether one is waiting or stalking, resting or grasping, God appears, offering a vision of "fleeing shreds ... the back parts ... a gift, an abundance."[47] The gift, however, is not so much a revelation of God as it is a revelation of the way to be in God's world—the way of being captured that Dillard herself captures in her Scriptural echo of Jacob, the grasping one at rest, who awakening cries, "'Surely the Lord is in this place; and I knew it not.'"[48]

Life then becomes something that is read in light of divine presence, and mystics join in the ancient chorus of those who make confession through spiritual autobiography. Dillard gathers her moments of reflection, the note cards of her days, and orders them for readers to tell the story of a soul.[49] One finds here not a linear plot but a recording of days, a series of moments. Her temporal movement from season to season corresponds to a mystical movement from kataphatic to apophatic experience. Yet, even here, such movement signifies not a progression of development but rather a gathering of the soul before God in all the moments of life. For Dillard, when the eternal in radical incarnation breaks into the meaningless temporal, the temporal is gathered in an eternal moment of meaning beyond understanding. Reading her spiritual autobiography, one may succumb to her narrative art. As Dillard relates her life experiences, her careful attending to life and mystery, she seeks to create mystical moments for the reader. Through the art of verbal allusion, Dillard creates an interpenetration of events, seeking to bring sudden insights of grace. One's way of reading then becomes one's way of living. One attends to the mystery: one lives in a world of contradictions and meaningless horror and yet is open to the radical possibility of God's incarnate presence in the midst of this world.

In a manner less overtly mystical yet certainly as artful, Merton constructs his autobiography by offering the reader moments of his life, scenes that he carefully constructs, through which one captures a glimpse of the divine. As he opens his autobiography, Merton posits a three-tiered experience of the world: one experiences the world as a captive, as an artist, or as a saint. All view the same world, all experience the same events, but captives see such events only through the eyes of the culture that surrounds them,[50] artists see them through eyes that have been opened by natural theology,[51] and saints see them through revealed theology and supernatural grace.[52] As Merton reflects upon his life, he invites the reader to see with the eyes of a saint. At critical moments, he suspends narrative action to offer his readers an artistic tableau.[53] These visual scenes, carefully constructed by a literary artist, invite contemplation, and, in such contemplation, one discovers ordinary life punctuated by the divine. Here, Merton's title, *The Seven Storey Mountain*, begins to make sense. His allusion to Dante's *Purgatorio* reveals his literary technique: as one journeys through the circular climb of purgatory toward the mystical vision, spiritual change is evoked by the contemplation of artistic tableaux. As Merton records the ordinary events of his life, he does so in a manner inviting contemplation: the scenes of ordinary life become transforming moments in spiritual autobiography. Through literary art, Merton trains his readers in the practices of close reading and, thereby, invites them to engage in spiritual contemplation. Through his example of spiritual autobiography, he forms others in the art of prayerfully reading their own lives in this world through the eyes of saints.[54]

In a manner still less overtly mystical and less artful, Price records his life experiences in a memoir that chronicles the temporal progression of his illness and healing. As he writes that narrative, however, Price also attends to the mystical wonder of life. He is at pains to argue that he is not mapping out his life according to some providential design: all that has happened "could have been some meaningless falling-domino chain of events. And if it was more—a fate intended and overseen by a force beyond me—who was I to attempt a precise map of the dark terrain? Only a blissed-out TV Bible hustler would dare reduce that weight of mystery to a trail of tea-leaves spelling a readable usable message."[55] Thus, Price maintains the paradoxical tension of a life of faith. While "God may consult you in unannounced moments ... He'll almost surely lurk beyond you in heavy drapery with face concealed."[56] Price denies discernment of a divine plan for life, but preserves the weight of divine mystery in life. He denies a divine message, but confesses a divine meaning. Mystical visions and locutions are valued then not for how they provide answers to life's questions but for how they propel one into the questionable possibilities of life.[57] Hence, Price at the end brings his readers to the "baffling God of Jews and Christians" who sets life and death before people and invites them to "choose life."[58] Regardless of how full of pain or suffering or the lack of meaning life may be, the possibility of the unknowable presence of God in life invites individuals to choose life in response to the divine.

Conclusion

Through spiritual life-writing, American mystics reveal their encounters with the divine. The focal field may be as large as creation or it may contract to a period of days. For each individual, however, American mystic spirituality involves the following: a paradoxical relationship with the church; an unexpected encounter with divine presence gracing a meaningless life with unknowable meaning; and a vibrant engagement with ordinary life, attentive to the mystery of God's presence in the world. At the heart of American mystic spirituality lies a holy freedom: God's radical freedom to act and the human's radical freedom to be.

American mysticism privileges God's freedom to act. God is free to be what God desires to be, not necessarily revealing his presence in the same way for everyone. Free to work outside of institutional structures, God is also free to work within such structures without being controlled by them or even recognized by those within them who believe in his work. This mystical experience of the divine, freely given, reveals that God is aware of the individual, granting the mystic an experience of his unknowable presence. Why God would be favorable to such individuals remains an unanswered question. This divine presence, however, does give unfathomable meaning to a meaningless life. Herein, American mystic spirituality privileges human freedom. Life is opened to the radical possibility of any experience to have divine meaning. From Dillard observing a goldfinch empty a purple thistle seedcase[59] to Merton remembering his childhood rejection of his younger brother John Paul,[60] any life experience may be the occasion when divine mystery breaks in.[61] The American mystic, therefore, attends to daily life in all of its variety with holy wonder. This radical freedom, both divine and human, transforms daily life into a life of active contemplation. God's radical freedom to be calls out of the human being a radical answer: all of one's meaningless experience has the potential of meaning beyond one's making and therefore is embraced in holy wonder. One lives in a blessed uncertainty, attending to all of life with wonder and awe.

In such reflection, individuals begin to form stories of God's work in their lives. They engage in spiritual life-writing, not necessarily with the pen but certainly with the tongue. Their stories may not be as overtly mystical as the experiences of Dillard or as all-encompassing as the writing of Merton, but with such stories they come to the church. For them, the sites and practices of the local congregation, even though once rejected, may still hold potential for divine revelation. There, American mystics begin to tell their stories in the presence of the local congregation. So pastors and parishioners discover themselves engaged in the art of divine hospitality with American mystics and holy conversations begin.

As with any conversation with a stranger, dialog brings discovery of both points that are strange to one's way of thinking or life experience and points that are of common interest. So it is with American mystic spirituality and the mind of Christ. On the one hand, beginning a conversation about life experience with an American mystic may bring one into contact with strange ways of interpreting God's work in the world. This essay has sought to alleviate some of that strangeness by offering an exploratory glimpse into the themes one encounters in the life-writing of American mystics. On the other hand, such conversations can bring up points of common interest, prodding the church to voice teachings long known but not always fully expressed. Suddenly, pastors and parishioners might find themselves rediscovering how to talk about the things of God: the radical freedom of God; the presence of the holy in their midst; what it means to encounter the certainty of divine presence in Jesus in a way that is beyond one's understanding; and the vibrant wonder of daily life as the Spirit works through creatures in God the Father's ordering of the world and mission therein.

At times such conversation will be awkward and tentative, as we search for the right words so that we faithfully express the mind of Christ to the American mystic. At other times, the conversation may be as familiar as the words of an old hymn, "Soul, Adorn Thyself with Gladness." Revised out of the Lutheran Service Book, Johann Franck's companion stanzas link the event of the Lord's Supper with a moment of mystical wonder:

In my heart I find ascending
Holy awe, with rapture blending,
As this mystery I ponder,
Filling all my soul with wonder,
Bearing witness at this hour
Of the greatness of God's power;
Far beyond all human telling
Is the power within Him dwelling.

Human reason, though it ponder,
Cannot fathom this great wonder
That Christ's body e'er remaineth
Though it countless souls sustaineth
And that He His blood is giving
With the wine we are receiving.
These great mysteries unsounded
Are by God alone expounded.[62]

Here, in an act of poetic devotion, Franck expresses wonder at the certain sacramental presence of Christ that lies beyond human understanding and teaches us ways of speaking that might further holy conversation with American mystics. An old hymn is surprisingly new when sung once again in our foreign land. Strangely, practicing the art of hospitality in conversation with the American mystic invites us who live with the mind of Christ to sing the old songs of God's hospitality, even to us, once again.

Endnotes

1 Richard Lischer, *Open Secrets* (New York: Broadway Books, 2001), 69–70.

2 Lischer, *Open Secrets*, 104.

3 These works include Annie Dillard's account of her Pittsburgh childhood, *An American Childhood*, and her Pulitzer Prize winning reflections on a two-year sojourn at Pilgrim Creek, *Pilgrim at Tinker Creek*; Thomas Merton's comprehensive spiritual autobiography, *The Seven Storey Mountain*; Kristin Ohlson's personal memoir of her interviews with the Poor Clares of Perpetual Adoration at St. Paul shrine in Cleveland, *Stalking the Divine*; and Reynolds Price's account of his childhood in North Carolina, *Clear Pictures: First Loves, First Guides*, and his memoir of his experience with debilitating cancer, *A Whole New Life: An Illness and a Healing*. The writers have been selected with a desire to be descriptive rather than comprehensive and exploratory rather than definitive. Much more could be written about contemporary American mystics and their spiritual life-writing before one then situates their experiences within the larger historical framework of American religious thought and experience. This particular essay simply seeks to begin a conversation, describing and exploring the patterns of thought and experience recorded in the life-writing of selected contemporary American mystics.

4 See F. Samuel Brainard, "Defining 'Mystical Experience,'" *Journal of the American Academy of Religion* 64 (Summer 1996): 359–393, and Sallie B. King, "Two Epistemological Models for the Interpretation of Mysticism," *Journal of the American Academy of Religion* 56 (Summer 1988): 257–279.

5 Annie Dillard, *An American Childhood* (New York: Harper & Row Publishers, 1987), 134.

[6] Dillard, *American Childhood*, 196–197.
[7] Ibid., 198–199.
[8] Ibid., 199.
[9] Kristin Ohlson, *Stalking the Divine* (New York: Penguin Group, 2003), 2.
[10] Ohlson, *Stalking*, 5–6.
[11] Ibid., 128; see also 139.
[12] Thomas Merton, *The Seven Storey Mountain* (New York: Harcourt Brace & Company, 1948), 47–48, 59, 111–112, and 119–125.
[13] Merton, *Seven Storey*, 94, 112, and 180–182.
[14] Ibid., 209–217.
[15] Ibid., 226.
[16] Ibid., 231.
[17] Ibid., 228.
[18] Ibid., 230.
[19] Ibid., 229.
[20] Merton, 346–348.
[21] Augustine, *The Confessions*, trans. Maria Boulding (New York: Vintage Books, 1997), 10.6, p. 201.
[22] Teresa of Avila, *The Life of Saint Teresa of Avila by Herself*, trans. J. M. Cohen (New York: Penguin Books, 1957), 208–209.
[23] Merton, 346–348.
[24] Reynolds Price, interview, "Common Boundary," quoted in Barbara Brown Taylor, *Home by Another Way* (Cambridge, Mass.: Cowley Publications, 1999), 138.
[25] Reynolds Price, *Clear Pictures* (New York: Ballantine Books, 1990), 262.
[26] For instance, consider his divine vision of Jesus by the Sea of Galilee or his divine locution of the single word "more" in *A Whole New Life: An Illness and a Healing* (New York: Scribner, 2003), 39–40, 42–46, and 80–82.
[27] Price, *Whole New Life*, 39.
[28] For example, see Price's *A Whole New Life: An Illness and a Healing, Letter to a Godchild: Concerning Faith, A Serious Way of Wondering: The Ethics of Jesus Imagined, Letter to a Man in the Fire: Does God Exist and Does He Care?, Clear Pictures: First Loves, First Guides, Honest Account of a Memorable Life: An Apocryphal Gospel*, and *The Three Gospels*.
[29] Price, *Clear Pictures*, 262–263.
[30] Price, *Whole New Life*, 42–43.
[31] Price, *Whole New Life*, 45.
[32] Ibid.
[33] Ibid., 81.
[34] Ibid.
[35] For Merton's trope of the mythical American hero, see *Seven Storey*, 14, 94, and 180–181.
[36] Merton, 181.
[37] Annie Dillard, *Pilgrim at Tinker Creek* (New York: HarperCollins Publishers, 1998), 9.
[38] Dillard, *Pilgrim*, 275.
[39] Dillard, *Pilgrim*, 78–104. For the specific allusions to grace as an archer, see 91 and 102.
[40] Ibid., 81.
[41] Ohlson, 181.
[42] Ibid., 215. While not receiving revelations, Ohlson reveals the mystical desires that fuel some individuals as they approach the local congregation and the spiritual practices of the faithful. By the close of her memoir, Ohlson discovers another avenue for spiritual formation or—social action. See pp. 235–236. In fact, one might read her work as a testimony to how a former Maoist and social activist sought spiritual growth through mystical practices only to discover a different avenue of devotion and growth in Christian acts of mercy for the poor.
[43] Price, *Whole New Life*, 54.
[44] Price, *Whole New Life*, 54–55.

[45] Dillard, *Pilgrim*, 104.
[46] Dillard, *Pilgrim*, 207.
[47] Ibid., 208.
[48] Ibid.
[49] See Dillard's reflections on the composition of *Pilgrim at Tinker Creek* in "Afterward to the Twenty-fifth Anniversary Edition," in *Pilgrim*, 278–282.
[50] For Merton, the heroic American myth and the culture fostered by film form the vision of the captive. While Merton plays out this myth in his own life experience, he also uses his grandparents as types of those who are captive to the American culture generated by film. See *Seven Storey*, 22–27 and 436.
[51] For Merton, the artist's vision is "a natural analogue of mystical experience," involving an intuitive perception of reality through natural theology. While Merton links his intellectual conversion to the development of the artist's vision, this vision is best typified in Merton's father who was an artist and in Merton's interest in literary studies, particularly William Blake. See *Seven Storey*, 3–4, 221, and 436.
[52] For Merton, the saint's vision is occasioned by God's mystical interventions that open the eyes of the individual to see the world through revealed theology and supernatural grace. Merton scatters such interventions throughout his life story, but reading them together one discovers that Merton reveals an experience of God, in Christ, in the church, intellectually in the church's teaching, and experientially in the church's sacraments. See *Seven Storey*, 116–124, 228–230, 245–246, 278–280, and 436–437.
[53] For example, see the parallel scenes of his interaction with his younger brother John Paul in *Seven Storey*, 25–26 and 438–439.
[54] As Merton records the story of his life in a way that draws others into contemplation, one could argue that he embodies contemplata aliis tradere, which he claims is "the height of the mystical life and of mystical experience," namely that "Christ living in us and directing all our actions might Himself draw men to desire and seek that same exalted union because of the joy and the sanctity and the supernatural vitality radiated by our example." See *Seven Storey*, 453–462, esp. 457–458.
[55] Price, *Whole New Life*, 176.
[56] Ibid., 185.
[57] Ibid., 184.
[58] Ibid., 185.
[59] Dillard, *Pilgrim*, 217–219.
[60] Merton, *Seven Storey*, 25–27.
[61] Technically, in spiritual autobiography, these writers highlight this ability of life experience to be read in different ways by the interplay of mimesis and diegesis. Through mimesis, the writers relate the bare life experience and, through diegesis, the writers evoke a sense of the divine mystery within that experience. So, for example, Merton may relate a life experience such as his rejection of his younger brother that, in the time of the narrative reveals the vision of a captive, but in recollection reveals the vision of a saint.
[62] Johann Franck, "Soul, Adorn Thyself with Gladness," trans. Catherine Winkworth, The Lutheran Hymnal (St. Louis: Concordia Publishing House, 1941), 305, vv. 5 and 6.

Science and Culture

Joel P. Okamoto

Science, Technology, and the American Mind

Introduction

Factors assumed to be essential to social well-being and national interest do much to shape and, indeed, to make up the "American Mind"—the complex of beliefs and values that give us in the United States the ways we recognize, understand, and assess ourselves, our lives, and the world we inhabit. These factors include "democracy" and "capitalism." Without freedom and free enterprise, without justice and economic opportunity for all, life might not even be worth living; at least they are worth fighting for. To question them would amount to questioning the American way of life. It is the same way with "science" and "technology." Without them, life might not even be worth fighting for; at least they are worth betting on for security and prosperity. To give up on them would amount to giving up on the American future.

These factors, especially as they bear on the American Mind, also should interest us Christians in the United States as we seek faithfully to lead lives and to witness to all that is true and good, especially to the Lordship of Jesus Christ and his return to judge the living and the dead. With that interest (and limits on space) in mind, I will focus on two sets of issues in which science and technology affect the American Mind. Certainly I could have dealt with other significant issues. But I have selected these because they touch closely and clearly on central Christian themes. They are 1) science and technology as sources of hope and reasons for fear, and 2) the impact of science on claims to truth.

Science and Technology as Sources of Hope and Reasons for Fear

Christians confess their God—the God and Father of Jesus Christ—to be the one true God and the maker of heaven and earth, and of all things visible and invisible. As such, we should rest our hopes entirely on him and his promises (this is justification by faith) and fear him above all else. Americans, however, commonly think of science and technology as significant sources of hope, and also occasionally as important reasons for fear, and so we may count them as false gods who compete for the hearts, minds, and lives of Americans—including American Christians.

It is easy to explain how Americans find both hope and fear in science and technology, because most Americans consider science and technology central ingredients of their lives—and nearly all act like they are, whether they know it or not. They are part of every child's education. They are intrinsic to the research, development, production, distribution, marketing, support, service, bureaucracy, and financial transactions that make up so many of today's businesses. They are vital to modern health care. They are essential to mass communications and popular entertainment. If you want to discuss most aspects of American society and culture, you can find a place for science and technology in the conversation.

Science and technology are sources of hope because they already have proven so useful and given us so much. Through scientific theories, discoveries, and methods, and with technological developments, we now have devices that light homes and cook food; telephones we talk with and computers that process information; cars we drive and planes we fly in; vaccines we give to prevent diseases and drugs we use to treat them. Science and technology, of course, are not *objects* that might be extended to a limit or resources that might be used up, but chiefly *methods* to expand reliably our knowledge and to extend efficiently our activity. As such they have secured an abundant and steadily improving life for Americans, and they give Americans confidence about dealing with and succeeding in the future. President George W. Bush reflected this confidence when he announced the "American Competitiveness Initiative" in 2006:

> My fellow Americans,
>
> One of the great engines of our growing economy is our Nation's capacity to innovate. Through America's investments in science and technology, we have revolutionized our economy and changed the world for the better. Groundbreaking ideas generated by innovative minds in the private and public sectors have paid enormous dividends—improving the lives and livelihoods of generations of Americans.

> To build on our successes and remain a leader in science and technology, I am pleased to announce the American Competitiveness Initiative... We know that as other countries build their economies and become more technologically advanced, America will face a new set of challenges. To ensure our continued leadership in the world, I am committed to building on our record of results with new investments—especially in the fields of physical sciences and engineering. Advances in these areas will generate scientific and technological discoveries for decades to come.[1]

Like his fellow Americans, President Bush assumed that science and technology are key to innovation; that innovation is key to continuing growth in the economy; and that a growing economy is key to improving the lives and livelihoods of future generations of Americans. He also assumed that other societies think alike and that Americans either must strive to keep up or get left behind.

Also like his fellow Americans, President Bush assumed American accomplishments and prospects, which are largely material or monetary and are tied to science and technology far more than to art or architecture, to music or literature, to philosophy or religion. Some will be quick to point out that this is because paintings and books and doctrines do not feed or shelter or clothe. But this explanation goes only so far for the American society, where accumulation for many runs well beyond "all that I need to support this body and life."

Just this much suggests that science and technology belong to the American pantheon. They are "gods" in the Large Catechism sense as things to which we look for all that is good and for protection against all that is harmful. If mammon—money and possessions—remains the most common idol on earth, then science and technology must stand close behind.

But science and technology bring out the issue of God and gods in another way: they hold out for us the even more radical promise of "playing God" by altering nature. Advancements in molecular biology already have permitted genetic modifications that could not come about otherwise. Prince Charles spoke for many when he said in a 1998 article, "I happen to believe that this kind of genetic modification takes mankind into realms that belong to God, and to God alone."[2]

It is at this point, too, that fears about science and technology become acute. As a child, I loved Homer Price stories, and I still remember fondly the stories of the Super-Duper, the automatic doughnut machine that wouldn't turn off, and "Experiment 13." This experiment, you might remember, consisted of mysterious seeds that grew into very large plants—weeds, to be exact. When their identity was finally discovered, panic ensued and violence was threatened before a bribe was made and Centerburg was saved from giant ragweed. The seeds of "Experiment 13" foreshadowed today's genetically modified crops, and the worries of Centerburg's citizens have been surpassed by the worries of the Prince of Wales, who feared that their effects on other crops, nature, and those who eat them are impossible to assess with a high degree of confidence and that any damage or corruption would be impossible to reverse, perhaps even to contain.

Other advances in science and technology pose equally serious risks. As Bill Joy, a noted computer scientist, pointed out in his much-discussed article entitled "Why the Future Doesn't Need Us," developments in genetics, nanotechnology, and robotics "are so powerful that they can spawn whole new classes of accidents and abuses."[3] Moreover, "for the first time, these accidents and abuses are widely within reach of individuals or small groups. They will not require large facilities or rare raw materials. Knowledge alone will enable use of them." What kind of accident might occur? The so-called "gray goo problem" is one:

> "Plants" with "leaves" no more efficient than today's solar cells could out-compete real plants, crowding the biosphere with an inedible foliage. Tough omnivorous "bacteria" could out-compete real bacteria: they could spread like blowing pollen, replicate swiftly, and reduce the biosphere to dust in a matter of days. Dangerous replicators could easily be too tough, small, and rapidly spreading to stop—at least if we make no preparation. We have trouble enough controlling viruses and fruit flies.
>
> Among the cognoscenti of nanotechnology, this threat has become known as the "gray goo problem." Though masses of uncontrolled replicators need not be gray or gooey, the term "gray goo" emphasizes that replicators able to obliterate life might be less inspiring that a single species of crabgrass...
>
> Gray goo would surely be a depressing ending to our human adventure on Earth, far worse than mere fire or ice, and one that could stem from a simple laboratory experiment. Oops.

The prospects of a modern day Frankenstein (or Dulcey Dooner) initiating a disaster like "gray goo" explain many fears about science and technology.

But hopes and fears of this kind are most intense when it comes to developments in science and technology involving human beings. Already such words as "cloning" and "embryonic stem cell research" stand for fiercely contested political issues and reflect both great hopes and great fears. They reflect the hope for treatments for terrible afflictions, for lengthening life, and for increasing our capacities. They reflect the fear that we may be altering human nature, that research will put the lives of unborn children in even greater peril, and that these developments will increase the gap between the rich, who can afford such treatments and enhancements, and the poor, who cannot.

Moreover, if Ray Kurzweil, a highly respected inventor and leading futurist, is correct, then genetic modifications will comprise only a brief intermediate step in human evolution toward a non-biological existence. Kurzweil bases this claim on the observation that the time between key breakthroughs has been decreasing *exponentially*. Even when one ignores the biological evolutionary events he counts, developments from agriculture to the wheel and writing to the printing press to the transistor and nuclear energy show an exponential (rather than linear) acceleration in technological progress.[4] Kurzweil concludes from this that humankind is approaching a threshold that will change not only our views on nearly everything—but also on life itself. Like all exponential curves, the initial rate of advance in science and technology was very slow and accelerated very slowly, too. But, like all exponential curves, it eventually will reach an inflection point, after which advances will succeed one another so quickly that the pace of change will seem to be exploding. He believes that we are near this point. He predicts that in the twenty-first century "the pace of technological change will be so rapid, its impact so deep, that human life will be irreversibly transformed."[5] He calls this approaching period "the Singularity." When it arrives, "the concepts that we rely on to give meaning to our lives, from our business models to the cycle of human life, including death itself" will be transformed radically and irreversibly.[6]

Although all aspects of life will be touched, the most momentous effect of "the Singularity" will be on human beings themselves. The Singularity will give humans the capacity to transcend the limitations and imperfections of their biological, "version 1.0" bodies and brains.[7] He estimates that by the 2030s human beings will be able to "upload" their brains onto a non-biological "computational substrate."[8] Eventually people will be able to transcend their biological bodies and brains ("version 1.0") altogether or as they see fit. Kurzweil recognizes that a key question is whether a new, nonbiological "Ray Kurzweil" or "Jane Smith" is fundamentally the same as the old, biological "Ray Kurzweil" or "Jane Smith." This question may be impossible to answer, but Kurzweil believes that it may be moot, because the transition from "version 1.0" to "version 2.0" and beyond will be gradual and largely unnoticed.[9] In any case, moreover, Kurzweil believes that this shift is already underway, that already "we are becoming cyborgs."[10]

Kurzweil claims that this vision of the future is neither utopian nor dystopian.[11] Nevertheless, he does regard it with *hope*, and he stresses the great potential that this future holds.

> We will gain power over our fates. Our mortality will be in our own hands. We will be able to live as long as we want (a subtly different statement from saying we will live forever). We will fully understand human thinking and will vastly extend and expand its reach. By the end of this century, the nonbiological portion of our intelligence will be trillions of trillions of times more powerful than unaided human intelligence.[12]

This vision takes the matter of "playing God" to its logical conclusion, and elsewhere, in a dialogue with Bill Gates, he makes this explicit. Gates says that he agrees "99 percent" with Kurzweil, but he finds his optimism "almost a religious faith." Kurzweil responds that a new religion actually is needed. Traditional religion's principal function, in his view, "has been to rationalize death," but in a post-biological existence, death will no longer be an issue, so traditional religion will have no place. This new religion would have two principles: respect for human consciousness (a "Golden Rule") and the importance of knowledge. But how would such a religion be advanced?

> Bill: So is there a God in this religion?
>
> Ray: Not yet, but there will be. Once we saturate the matter and energy in the universe with intelligence, it will "wake up," be conscious, and sublimely intelligent. That's about as close to God as I can imagine.[13]

Of course, either way, this claim is remarkable—remarkable as a source of hope or remarkable as a reason to fear.

Science and the Truth about the World

Both science and technology do more than give Americans something to think about and reasons for hope and fear. They also inform *how* Americans think. With technology, questions of this sort have been asked at least since Plato related Socrates' story about Theuth and Thamus in the *Phaedrus*. According to this story, Theuth was showing his inventions to Thamus. When it came to letters, his greatest invention, Thamus concluded that they would lead to forgetfulness and lead people away from being truthful and wise. Contemporary successors to this line of thinking and concern would include Aldous Huxley (*Brave New World*), and Marshall McLuhan and Neil Postman, both of whom wrote about the effects of media on minds, and the pediatrician who warned one of my children, "Television makes you stupid." With science, Christians find it a competitor in claims to truth about the universe and everything in it.

Most Americans will agree that modern science has added to our knowledge of the universe. Relatively few actually can explain much of this knowledge well, but ignorance is no obstacle to the belief that we know much more about the universe than people did when the Pilgrims landed or at the time of the Revolutionary War, and that it makes our lives more comfortable, healthy, and secure than they ever could have imagined. But science has done more than add to our knowledge of the universe; it has changed radically *how we view the universe and understand our place in it.*

Above all, this is a result of the Copernican revolution. Copernicus's hypothesis began as a proposal to improve astronomical calculations, but his proposal raised questions and problems the working through of which brought about a more general "scientific revolution." Among these developments, Newton's theory of gravitation was the most significant achievement. Today most of us do not appreciate what Newton's accomplishments meant at his time, but philosopher Karl Popper helps us to sense what those who lived shortly after Newton, and saw his theory vindicated in every respect, would have felt:

> After the unmatched daring with which the Ancients had tackled the riddle of the Universe there had come long periods of decay and recovery, and then a staggering success. Newton had discovered the long sought secret... No qualified judge of the situation could doubt any longer that Newton's theory was true. It had been tested by the most precise measurements, and it had always been right. It had led to the prediction of minute deviations from Kepler's laws, and to new discoveries. In a time like ours, when theories come and go like the buses in Piccadilly, and when every schoolboy has heard that Newton has long been superseded by Einstein, it is hard to recapture the sense of conviction which Newton's theory inspired, or the sense of elation, and of liberation. A *unique event* had happened in the history of thought, one which could never be repeated: the first and final discovery of the absolute truth about the universe. An age-old dream had come true. Mankind had obtained *knowledge*, real, certain,

> indubitable, and demonstrable knowledge—divine *scientia* or *episteme*, and not merely *doxa*, human opinion.[14]

To be sure, as Popper intimates and as he would explore elsewhere with penetrating insight, later investigation would lead to doubts about features of Newton's theory and then to Einstein's theory of gravitation. But for two centuries, Newton's theory was considered *truth*, and for very good reasons.

> The almost universal belief that Newton's theory *must* be true was not only understandable but seemed to be well-founded. Never had there been a better theory, nor one more severely tested... Moreover, it was one of the triumphs of Newtonian theory that it stood up to subsequent observations which as regards precision went far beyond what could be attained in Newton's own time... Newton's theory had made the most astonishing and exact predictions, all of which had proved strikingly correct. Only ignorant men could doubt its truth.[15]

And so, Newton's theory became "a dogma of almost stupefying power."[16]

Although the most eminent, Newton's theory was only one of several notable accomplishments, and together they comprised the scientific revolution.[17] With these scientific discoveries and theories, it was as if a key had been found to unlock the door to knowledge of the universe, or as if a light powerful enough to reach into the heavens had been handed over and switched on. Modern science not only greatly expanded knowledge of the universe, but it also promised to continue to expand this knowledge. Science gave us a new picture of the universe, but, even more importantly, it also gave us a new way to picture the universe. It gave us not only a new and fascinating look, but also a powerful means to keep on looking and discovering.

Its accounts of the universe were supported by such seemingly sure demonstrations and obtained by such powerful methods—put in a theological idiom, they *revealed* so much—that traditional religion—which meant especially Christianity—was forced to respond, almost always defensively. This defensiveness extended beyond physics to all the natural sciences, including chemistry, astronomy, and biology. Liberal theology characteristically gave ground, while conservative theology responded in two typical ways: 1) by responding in kind, trying to show that Christian claims were compatible with science, or 2) by withdrawing, emphasizing the discontinuity between science and religion. In all cases, however, science has emerged as a competitor to religion; culturally it has gained the upper hand in the United States, and religion has been put on the defensive.

Science, however, has gained an advantage not only because of the *power* of its theories, discoveries, and methods, but also in terms of its *virtue*. Science has the virtue of being open to criticism.

Many people do not fully appreciate this feature. They believe that the "empirical method" sets science apart, which they understand as a method that begins with observations, proceeds to theories, and is supported by confirmations. But this account of science cannot make a key distinction: it cannot distinguish between what most would regard as a genuine science, like astronomy, and what most would regard as a pseudo-science, like astrology. Both begin with observations; both proceed to theories; and both can show evidence that *confirms* or *verifies* their theories. So this account of science fails to make precisely the distinction that any adequate account of science must make.

In the middle of the twentieth century, Karl Popper supplied a more viable account. He held that a properly "scientific" theory is one that can conceivably be *falsified*. Popper came to realize that confirmations or verifications are not crucial in distinguishing "science" from "pseudo-science" or "metaphysics," as was usually thought. Instead it was the *possibility of refutation or falsification* that set scientific theories apart from pseudo-scientific and metaphysical ones.[18] The difference between astronomy and astrology is not that one has confirmations and the other does not (they both do). They differ in that acknowledged astronomical theories are put in a way that leaves them open to being refuted (they just have not yet been), but astrological ones cannot be refuted. This insight led Popper to his famous saying: "A theory that is not refutable by any conceivable event is non-scientific. Irrefutability is not a virtue of a theory (as many people think), but a vice."[19]

Irrefutability is an issue with astrology and alchemy, and also with the stories, doctrines, and positions of most, if not all, religions. When disagreements and conflicts break out, irrefutability becomes a problem—and refutability a virtue. Perhaps the American Founding Fathers intuitively grasped this problem when they legally forbade the establishment of any religion. This problem, in any case, has led to excluding most kinds of religious doctrines and references from normative (as opposed to descriptive or comparative) teaching in public schools (justified by the First Amendment). Refutability in a claim or a doctrine, on the other hand, has special value and validity in just such a situation. So, when science is pitted against religion, it has not only power and, in the American situation, religious neutrality, but also virtue in its favor.

Power, religious neutrality, and virtue make a formidable combination. So it is no wonder that science exerts such influence on the

American Mind, and that Americans are disposed to a scientific explanation or to evidence drawn from a scientist's experiment.

This influence is more far-reaching than often realized. We can see this in the ongoing debate over the science curriculum in public schools. On one side advocates of teaching divine creation in public schools argue that "evolution" is a theory and not a fact, that it is "bad science" to call evolution a fact, and that many scientists and teachers of science confuse "science" and "metaphysics." On the other side, opponents of teaching divine creation in these schools argue that "evolution" is an established fact, that it would be a mistake to regard "intelligent design theory" as scientific, and that it is important not to confuse science with religion or philosophy. Ironically, advocates of teaching divine creation show just how deeply science affects how any American may think. They reflect an unreflective embrace of science. This embrace explains why "creationism" is now advanced as a theory of "intelligent design" and why "intelligent design" is put forward as a "scientific" theory. It also explains why it matters so much that the topic of an intelligent designer belongs in the "science" curriculum, why "creation science" has developed, and why a museum—an Enlightenment institution—for creation has opened recently. Even those who take a stand against a particular scientific theory, or against a misplaced confidence in science, usually think and act according to many modern scientific beliefs and values.

But it should be pointed out that a theory or set of theories as sweeping and powerful as Newton's theories of gravitation and mechanics or Darwin's theory of evolution stand for more than just an explanation. They serve as exemplars for other investigations and act as symbols for sets of shared assumptions, conventions, and aims for all those involved. Thomas Kuhn labeled these "paradigms."[20] They are not subject to simple confirmation or refutation, and they do not come and go in stages of orderly, rational progress, but rise and fall in "revolutions." These paradigms *give* problems and *enable* the hypotheses, experiments, and analyses that make up "normal science," which *do* proceed along careful, orderly, rational lines. Imre Lakatos offered a somewhat similar concept with his idea of a "scientific research programme," as did Karl Popper with the concept of a "metaphysical research programme." This was "not a testable scientific theory" but "a possible framework for testable scientific theories." The old Ptolemaic *paradigm*, for instance, was repeatedly shown to be inadequate in one respect or another, but for a long time, the theory itself was corrected and refined to accommodate discrepancies rather than abandoned entirely, until so many difficulties arose that it could not be sustained. Put in theological terms, the paradigm created *faith* and faith sustained the paradigm, until it could not be believed upon any longer—and a new one arose and created faith.

Concepts like "paradigm," "scientific research programme," and "metaphysical research programme" help to see more clearly the issue over evolution. A key point in the public debate is whether the theory is testable and, therefore, scientific. Many opponents and critics of evolution argue that it is not, while proponents argue that it is. In its booklet *Science, Evolution, and Creationism*, the National Academy of Sciences held, as Popper might well have put it, that "Any scientific explanation has to be *testable*—there must be possible observational consequences that could support the idea *but also ones that could refute it*."[21] On this basis, it argued that evolution was indeed scientific but that creationism and intelligent design theory were not. But Popper, among others, showed that it is irrefutable and, therefore, "metaphysics" according a distinction that he not only conceived of but that the National Academy of Sciences itself and many others hold. He explained:

> It is metaphysical because it is not testable. One might think that it is. It seems to assert that, if ever on some planet we find life which satisfies [the conditions of heredity and variation], then [natural selection] will come into play and bring about in time a rich variety of distinct forms. Darwinism, however, does not assert as much as this. For assume that we find life on Mars consisting of exactly three species of bacteria with a genetic outfit similar to that of three terrestrial species. Is Darwinism refuted? By no means. We shall say that these three species were the only forms among the many mutants which were sufficiently well adjusted to survive. And we shall say the same if there is only one species (or none). Thus Darwinism does not really *predict* the evolution of variety. It therefore cannot really *explain* it.[22]

But we should be clear that identifying the theory of evolution as "metaphysical" and not "scientific" is according to only one definition of science. It is a highly regarded definition, but also a specialized one, and one that does not rule out other legitimate senses of "science." Indeed, as just discussed, what we ordinarily and usefully call "science" includes more than testable theories. We can see that "science" includes the "paradigms" for "normal science" and "metaphysical research programmes" that serve as frameworks to work out scientific theories. So identifying evolutionary theory as "metaphysical" on precisely the terms that others use to identify the theory as "scientific" takes away one reason *not* to deal seriously with creationism and theories of intelligent design.[23] They cannot be ignored or pushed to the margins *simply* because they are not "scientific," because, by the same standard, we can and should say the same about the theory of evolution. By the same token, no one should expect many to have second thoughts about the validity of the theory of evolution simply because it cannot be classified as "scientific" according to a philosophical theory. No metaphysical theory or account is either false or meaningless simply because it is metaphysical. Indeed, it still may be true, and it may be able to explain much. Popper specifically calls the theory of evolution "invaluable," because without it we could not know certain things:

> I do not see how, without it, our knowledge could have grown as it has done since Darwin. In trying to explain experiments with bacteria which become adapted to, say, penicillin, it is quite clear that we are greatly helped by the theory of natural selection. Although it is metaphysical, it sheds much light upon very concrete and very practical researches. It allows us to study adaptation to a new environment (such as a penicillin-infested environment) in a rational way: it suggests the existence of a mechanism of adaptation, and it allows us even to study in detail the mechanism at work. And it is the only theory so far which does all that.[24]

So, in the debate over evolution and about all sciences, the question concerning metaphysics is not *whether* but *how* the "theory" is "metaphysical." Here it is clear that the method of science is atheistic (i.e., it is *methodologically* atheistic). Regardless of the particular discipline, it requires purely natural causes and effects (i.e., it is "naturalistic"). God, the devil, and angels, if they are to be included at all in a theory, must be available for observation and testing; if not, then they cannot be considered.

This naturalism is not necessarily a problem, but it becomes an issue in two related respects. The first respect concerns *truth*. Where the findings and theories of science seem to go against an explanation based on or consistent with a different metaphysical account, as evolution does against divine creation, a conflict over truth arises, and some kind of resolution or accommodation needs to be made. The second respect concerns *faith*. Naturalism is an issue when science is *believed* to provide an ultimate explanation and, therefore, excludes other kinds of explanations. This happens when religion itself is criticized, as Richard Dawkins does in his book *The God Delusion*.[25] But this happens also when religion and science are held to deal with two different realms of life and thought. We might call this an attempt at polytheism, because it tries to find a place for two (or more) gods, that is, two ultimate authorities. Steven Jay Gould did this when he called religion and science two "nonoverlapping magisteria," and the National Academy of Sciences did this in *Science, Evolution, and Creationism* when it claimed:

> Science and religion are based on different aspects of human experience. In science, explanations *must* be based on evidence drawn from examining the natural world. Scientifically

> based observations or experiments that conflict with an explanation eventually *must* lead to modification or even abandonment of that explanation. Religious faith, in contrast, does not depend only on empirical evidence, is not necessarily modified in the face of conflicting evidence, and typically involves supernatural forces or entities. Because they are not a part of nature, supernatural entities cannot be investigated by science. In this sense, science and religion are separate and address aspects of human understanding in different ways. Attempts to pit science and religion against each other create controversy where none needs to exist.[26]

This issue is complicated when those who believe in science as a final authority do not acknowledge the metaphysical dimension of their convictions, that is, they do not admit their *faith*.

The American Mind and Christian Life and Witness

Further discussion is needed on other issues concerning science, technology, and the American Mind, but I will draw this discussion to a close with a few comments about faithful Christian life and witness in the context of the influence and stature of science and technology in the United States.

The power and promise that science and technology have brought to American lives make them attractive idols, even to Christians. We saw this problem first with the blessings (and even the curses) that science and technology bring to our lives. One response is to follow the Large Catechism on the First Commandment, identify these idols, and call for repentance and faithfulness. But what does faithfulness look like? Here we might follow the Catechisms on the First Article and the Lord's Prayer. They stress that God is the Creator, who not only made us and all creatures but also provides all that we need for our lives, that is, who gives us our daily bread. Accordingly, they call on us to "thank and praise, serve and obey him," and also to trust in and look to God in the First Commandment sense as one who gives us good things and protects us from evil, praying "Our Father who art in heaven." Doing this, of course, is living by faith—that is, living out our justification by grace. Teaching and urging this life is, then, a basic responsibility of churches and their ministers.

Living by faith—and proclaiming the promises that give people something in which to put their faith and on which to place their hopes—is also the key response to the fears that science and technology evoke. Science and technology are so pervasive and powerful that there is nothing an individual or, likely, even an entire nation can do to secure itself against the problems suggested by Prince Charles and Bill Joy. God alone can do something about the threat. The good news lies in his promise actually to do it by raising the dead and giving them lives in the new creation. Just as science and technology lead Christians to consider protological matters ("I believe in God the Father Almighty, maker of heaven and earth"), so also they lead Christians to look forward to eschatological promises ("the resurrection of the body and the life everlasting").

Furthermore, living by faith means living contentedly. Science and technology combine with economics to foster desires and to promote discontent. True contentment is a fruit of the Spirit, but striving for contentment is a mandate for the Christian life, and encouraging it is now a basic pastoral responsibility. This is especially true when it comes to ourselves. As we saw, advances in science and technology promise radical changes to our bodies and minds and even the possibility of a "transhuman" or "post-biological" existence. Whether or not these speculations actually come to pass, they do ask Christians whether we can be content with the bodies and the capacities God gave us.

But we saw also that science can be regarded as metaphysics. In one way, if science is seen as a set of beliefs and values about a certain activity, it is not necessarily a problem for Christians. But in another way, when being "metaphysical" means providing the ultimate explanation for everything, science acquires a religious character and serves as another god. We should appreciate that it has shown itself to be a powerful and righteous god—powerful in that it explains so much and yields such benefits, and righteous in that it seems to act fairly and reasonably.

From the days of Galileo on, Christians have failed to appreciate the power and virtue of science, and for this reason have weakened their witness and credibility in general, and not just on topics like cosmology. Neil Postman brought this out when he argued that, beyond the issue of explaining the world, both religion and science share a common interest in controlling information. When wrestling with Copernican and Darwinian theories, Christians were contending for control—and lost.

> The Bible gives manifold instructions on what one must do and must not do, as well as guidance on what language to avoid (on pain of committing blasphemy), what ideas to avoid (on committing heresy), what symbols to avoid (on pain of committing idolatry). Necessarily but perhaps unfortunately, the Bible also explained how the world came into being in such literal detail that it could not accommodate new information produced by the telescope and subsequent

> technologies. The trials of Galileo and, three hundred years later, of Scopes were therefore about the admissibility of certain kinds of information. Both Cardinal Bellarmine and William Jennings Bryan were fighting to maintain the authority of the Bible to control information about the profane world as well as the sacred. In their defeat, more was lost than the Bible's claim to explain the origins and structure of nature. The Bible's authority in defining and categorizing moral behavior was also weakened.[27]

So Christians should learn and respect the fact that science has attained what I call "power" and "virtue" in its explanations and methods. Power and virtue lend authority and prestige to science, especially over religious and philosophical accounts, conclusions, and teachings. One reason that Christians in particular find this difficult is that they often do not have good reasons for their own accounts, conclusions, and teachings. They may have won the battles with Galileo and Scopes, but are losing the war.

Most especially, as Postman's account implies, Christians need to deal with the problem of biblical authority. The Bible is the Word of God, and we can and should say that it is inspired, but this confession can do little work in supporting our account of the universe, our conclusions about life, and all of our teachings. The doctrine of inspiration arose to defend a certain way of interpreting the Scriptures, not to show their origins or authority. That kind of account depends on the identity of Jesus as the Christ and the Son of God, which was called into question by his crucifixion but justified in his resurrection, and on those commissioned to speak in his name and testify to him and his God. To be sure, this account will not provide a decisive, irrefutable argument against other accounts, but it will offer fundamental reasons for our positions and our lives and lend credibility for our witness to Americans and the world.

Endnotes

1 George W. Bush, February 2, 2006. Accessed from http://georgewbush-whitehouse.archives.gov/stateoftheunion/2006/aci/index.html
2 "The Seeds of Disaster," The Daily Telegraph, 8 June 1998.
3 Bill Joy, "Why the Future Doesn't Need Us," *Wired* 8, no. 4 (April 2000). Accessed from http://www.wired.com/wired/archive/8.04/joy.html. All quotations in this paragraph are from this article.
4 Ray Kurzweil, *The Singularity Is Near: When Humans Transcend Biology* (New York: Viking, 2005), 13–18.
5 Ibid., 7.
6 Ibid.
7 Ibid., 9.
8 Ibid., 199.

[9] Ibid., 202.
[10] Ibid., 309.
[11] Ibid., 7.
[12] Ibid., 9.
[13] Ibid., 374–375.
[14] Karl Popper, "Nature of Philosophical Problems," in *Conjectures and Refutations: The Growth of Scientific Knowledge*, Routledge Classics edition (London and New York: Routledge, 2002), 125. Emphasis original.
[15] Karl Popper, "On the Status of Science and of Metaphysics," in *Conjectures and Refutations: The Growth of Scientific Knowledge*, Routledge Classics edition (London and New York: Routledge, 2002), 250, 251, 258. Emphasis original.
[16] Ibid., 258.
[17] For instance, see the examples that Kant cited in the Preface to the second edition *Critique of Pure Reason*:

> When Galileo caused balls, the weights of which he had himself previously determined, to roll down an inclined plane; when Torricelli made the air carry a weight which he had calculated beforehand to be equal to that of a definite volume of water; or in more recent times, when Stahl changed metals into oxides, and oxides back into metal, by withdrawing something and then restoring it, a light broke upon all students of nature.

Immanuel Kant, "Preface to Second Edition," in *Critique of Pure Reason*, trans. Norman Kemp Smith (New York: Macmillan & Co., Ltd., 1929), 20.
[18] Karl Popper, "Science: Conjectures and Refutations," in *Conjectures and Refutations: The Growth of Scientific Knowledge*, Routledge Classics edition (London and New York: Routledge, 2002), 44.
[19] Ibid., 48.
[20] Thomas S. Kuhn, *The Structure of Scientific Revolutions*, 3rd ed. (Chicago and London: The University of Chicago Press, 1996).
[21] National Academy of Sciences and Institute of Medicine of the National Academies, Science, Evolution, and Creationism (Washington D.C.: The National Acadamies Press, 2008), 10.
[22] Karl Popper, Unended Quest, 198–199.
[23] I am using "metaphysical" in a broad sense that would include the accounts of various religions.
[24] Ibid., 199–200.
[25] Richard Dawkins, *The God Delusion* (Boston and New York: Houghton Mifflin, 2006).
[26] Stephen Jay Gould, "Nonoverlapping Magisteria," *Natural History* 106 (March 1997): 16–22; Science, Evolution, and Creationism, 12.
[27] Neil Postman, *Technopoly: The Surrender of Culture to Technology* (New York: Vintage Books, 1993), 77–78.

David I. Lewis

Cinema and the American Mind

Introduction

Any serious effort to understand what constitutes the American mind should, among other aspects of American life, take into account that realm which is known as "American popular culture." A discussion of American popular culture would inquire how and to what degree this culture reflects the beliefs, knowledge, attitudes, ideas, and experiences of the people of this country. Then, to the degree that the popular culture reflects the worldview of "popular America," we can perceive some of what beliefs, knowledge, attitudes, ideas, and experiences comprise the American mind. Any discussion of American popular culture must then include a consideration of the medium of film.

Film could well be called the defining medium of American popular culture of the twentieth century as well as the one medium through which American popular culture has exerted great influence outside of its borders.[1] Moviemaking, of course, has not been limited to American film production, nor have American films been made in isolation of the wider international scene. Even as they have exerted their own influence abroad, American films have also been greatly influenced by foreign films. Not only this, but in the pantheon of the great directors of American film there are several foreign-born auteurs (e.g., Fritz Lang and Alfred Hitchcock) who had careers in their home countries before (and sometimes after) working in the United States. A simple consideration of film distribution, however, shows that American films have been the most watched films on a worldwide scale and that for nearly a century now the United States has been the premier producer and distributor of films.[2] What is more, for the sake of the discussion here, it is the American film that would more naturally help to identify an American worldview, for these are the films that Americans make and that Americans are watching.[3]

This paper will consider American cinema as one means through which to identify, understand, discuss, and critique the American mind—those beliefs, knowledge, attitudes, ideas, and experiences that in part define Americans and their culture. Various approaches to film theory will be considered, and this will be done especially to see how it is argued that films *reflect* the worldview of the cultures that produce them. After considering film theory, this paper will examine how the worldview of the classical era of Hollywood filmmaking (1929–1967) is outlined and described by practitioners of the Ideological approach to film theory and how this approach would identify an ideology—the so-called "American capitalist ideology"—which underlies films of that era. This paper will then show how two great directors of the classical era, John Ford and Frank Capra, each in a film arguably seen as one of his best, Ford's *The Searchers* and Capra's *It's a Wonderful Life*, offered a critique of and a response to this very same ideology even at the very time it is said by the theorists to have dominated the Hollywood studio system.

This study of film may then provide some basis for a discussion of how the "American mind" as exemplified in Hollywood films of the classical era may be critiqued in light of the faith and life to which the Church is called. Perhaps American cinema does provide one lens into those beliefs, knowledge, attitudes, ideas, and experiences that constitute the American mind. By considering this the Church may better understand what may be true and good in this worldview, but also how in light of our calling we are to live in confession *against* many of these beliefs, attitudes, and ideas. Because of the scope of the subject matter, this paper will limit its examination to the ideology of films of the classical era of filmmaking.

Theory: Film—Affective or Reflective (or Both)

When considering the role of cinema in discussing the American worldview, two issues arise. The first issue is whether and then to what degree films are *affective*, that is, whether they can shape the beliefs, knowledge, attitudes, ideas, and experiences of their viewers and, if so, how they do this. The primary goal of most films is to entertain, but this does not in and of itself eliminate the fact that any given film may also inform, educate, and even manipulate its viewers even while entertaining them. And so with this question cultural observers may then also discuss how this effect should be evaluated—as neutral, beneficial, or pernicious. The second issue, then, is whether and then to what degree films are *reflective* of the beliefs, knowledge, attitudes, ideas, and experiences of their producers and/or their viewers. With this question, films could be used as a sort of lens through which cultural observers would look to determine the values of the culture that produces them.

Film theory from its beginning seems to have viewed these two questions as somewhat mutually exclusive—film either affects or reflects.[4] The truth, however, is more possibly that film, especially great film, accomplishes both tasks at the same time and that the history of American cinema involves an ongoing hermeneutical spiral in which films both reflect the American worldview even as they may affect the American audience in ways that could, depending on the film, reinforce, challenge, or perhaps modify that worldview. (In this discussion one could then also consider various views that a major front of the so-called "culture war" taking place in the United States today is fought in the realm of popular culture, and that it is here that the "Hollywood elite" promulgate a worldview that actually reflects their own ideology and that is at odds with the ideology of mainstream America and traditional American values.[5])

In this section I will consider various approaches toward film theory and how these may provide some insight into how and in what ways film can be affective and reflective. In general, film theory tries to understand film as a unique art form and then provide a conceptual framework in which to understand a film's relationship to reality, the individual viewers, and society at large.[6]

Reflectionism

One question that arose early in the history of cinema was whether or not film should even be considered an art form. Anthony Easthope notes that from the beginning film has had the capacity to stun audiences because of its "seeming capacity to reproduce reality transparently, immediately, directly."[7] Early audiences of film had never experienced anything like these moving pictures before. Viewers of *The Great Train Robbery* (1903) were said to have screamed and tried to move out of the way in response to a scene which depicted an oncoming locomotive.[8] Because of this "seeming realism," it could be argued that film cannot be considered a true form of art when evaluated according to Kantian aesthetics. According to Immanuel Kant, a proper approach to art should distinguish between sensation and contemplation. True art is not so much what can be sensed, but what can be contemplated by an observer, and the observer must therefore be detached from the object under consideration. Only when the observer is detached from the object could it then be evaluated as aesthetically pleasing for its own sake and not for any sort of usefulness or social purpose. Key to this aesthetic is the ability of the viewer to remain detached and uninvolved.[9]

The nature of film would seem naturally to violate this aesthetic. In film the viewer becomes involved in an experience which appears to be real and thus from which the viewer cannot so easily remain uninvolved and detached. The events portrayed by the moving pictures pass so quickly that there is no time for the sensation to be processed and contemplated. It can only be experienced. As such, the argument could be (and was) that film was not true art, but rather only "the feeble machinations of real life."[10] What is more, such a medium could then too easily be used for social propaganda, to manipulate the viewer's understanding of the world.[11]

The earliest film theorists attempted to defend film as a legitimate form of art by stressing first that each film stands alone in its own right as a unique creation of the artist. A film is not a reflection of reality outside of the film in the real world, but a construction which uses the raw materials of reality to form its own unique reality in the world of the film. With such a view it was then argued that films are more reflective than affective, though here what they are said to reflect is a constructed reality put together by the artists by means of the equipment. That a film is a construction of reality would allow the viewer the capacity to remain critically detached. This earliest theoretical approach to film analysis is known as Formalism (or Creationism).[12] This approach argued that film was not simply a representation of real events, but that each film was a construction of its own reality that a viewer could never witness as such in real life. Such theorists would note and evaluate how the various techniques used to make a film—to include camera angles, lighting, framing, and editing—do not simply represent reality, *but construct it*. The experience of the person viewing this construction is thus different than the way in which that person would view reality. The viewer encounters the film in the cinema, seeing two-dimensional images on a flat screen, a screen which, in turn, limits the frame of reference. This is not "real life." Thus each film brings to life its own world—and thus each film is a unique work of art.[13] Formalism was a dominant theory from the age of silent movies until about 1970.[14]

One reaction to Formalism was the Realist theory. In *seeming* opposition to the formalists, the realists stressed that the very virtue of film was the powerful resemblance that photography has to reality, that the viewer is forced to accept as real what the photograph (or moving photographs) "re-presents." It is through its apparent realism that film makes its affect upon the viewer and in this way film has a certain distinction and advantage over other artistic mediums. Thus with this approach there could be a bit more emphasis placed on how films are affective.[15] Nevertheless, the realists would argue too that "cinematic reality" is not so real that a viewer is unable to remain somewhat critically detached, especially when obvious attempts are made to manipulate his understanding.[16]

In spite of apparent differences in focus, both of these theories—Formalism and Realism—together posited the view that film must be assessed in part as a "mechanical reproduction," a progression of shots and frames. Because of this, these two theories are said to espouse what has been called Reflectionism, which states that in order to understand film one must see it is a series of photographic images which either reflect reality (Realism) or reflect a constructed reality (Formalism).[17] With these understandings in mind, it was argued, especially by Formalism, that one viewing a film can remain critically detached from it. This ability of the viewer to remain detached would then render film as a true art form. As such, the effect of the film upon the viewer was played down by both theories (though especially by Formalism).[18] Again, it is important to note that a fundamental purpose underlying both theories was the effort to defend cinema as an art form when evaluated in terms of the Kantian aesthetics.

The Ideological Theory

The Ideological theory emerged in the late 1960s and 1970s and became the first theory of film to be taken up as a serious field of academic study at the university level. Contra Formalism and Realism, the Ideological approach would not see film as "a series of photographic images that reproduce some reality" and from which the viewers can remain critically detached. This approach would instead see film primarily as speech—signs signifying a conceptual signified in a specific context in an attempt to affect meaning. *That this speech is made through the use of photographic images does not change the fact that it is speech.*[19]

The Ideological approach was influenced by various outside theories that were brought together for a more holistic approach to film: *Semiotics* contributed to the focus on film as text with various signs making meaning in the context of this larger text. Focus was now placed upon the entire film and not merely the mechanics or individual frames of photographs that go into making this film: one must understand the whole to understand the parts, and not the other way around. *Literary theory*, especially structuralism, contributed to a focus upon the function of narrative in a film. *Marxist theory* contributed to a focus upon how a film reflects the political and ideological superstructure determined by the economy in which it is produced. *Psychoanalysis* contributed to a focus upon a film's "intense effect" upon the spectators. Focus here was upon the psychological factors involved in viewing a film: in drawing the viewer into the film as into a mirror, the viewer is caused to revert to the symbolic stage of development ("children recognizing themselves in the mirror for the first time") and thus is brought to identify narcissistically with the main character of the film. The result is that the viewer identifies with the experiences of that character as if they were the viewer's own experiences.[20]

Influenced by these ultimate forms of modernist theory (and apparently lacking any concern to defend film as art according to Kantian aesthetics), the Ideological approach could attempt to explain how films are both reflective and affective: first, films reflect the worldview and value system of humankind in general (semiotics and structuralism), but then also in a unique way they reflect the worldview and values of the culture that produces them (Marxist theories). In reflecting these values film can then become a lens by which to understand the values of both its producers and its intended viewers, values which would be reflected by any film where both the producers and the viewers could be *unaware* of what is going on as they both produce and view these films. At the same time, especially considering the influence of psychoanalysis in this approach, one could also evaluate how films affect the viewer as well, shaping his understanding. Perhaps one could posit that a hermeneutical spiral is said to be in effect: a film not only reflects certain values universal to humanity and/or the dominant ideology of the culture that produces it, but it also then affects the viewer by reinforcing (or sometimes tweaking?) these beliefs, knowledge, understanding, attitudes, ideas, and experiences. Overall, especially with its use of psychology, but even also with its use of semiotics, structuralism and narrative analysis, and Marxism, this approach appears especially to stress how films make meaning, how they are affective. Only then does it become a theory that allows the student of cinema to use film as a lens to see what the worldview underlying the film might be.[21]

The Ideological approach seems to have remained the dominant theory in film studies. Nevertheless, it has been critiqued by various other approaches that have not sought so much to overthrow it as to modify it. One key critique is that the Ideological approach basically understands film through the perspective of only one type of viewer—what can ultimately be identified as the heterosexual white male—as if this viewer's experience is the defining experience of the entire culture. Films then can be viewed as not only reflecting certain values, but also of perpetuating certain power structures (i.e., those favorable to heterosexual white males). Modified theories thus would posit models of deconstructing classical films in order to bring about alternate understandings of these films and new ways of viewing them. These modified theories could further argue for new approaches to filmmaking which would intentionally place at the center other characters—characters who are not heterosexual, white, or male—and then tell the story from these other characters' point of view. And thus—in response to "classic" Ideologists—there are also feminist theories, various minority theories, gay and lesbian theories, and queer theories of film.[22]

The Auteur Theory

Somewhat varied from the Ideological approach is the theory that great directors can affect meaning through their unique skills and personality. This approach is referred to as the Auteur theory. According to this approach, a first premise is that great directors are to be considered the primary authors of their films. In this theory, then, one is not so much interested in how the film reflects the ideology of the culture, but how the director himself leaves his own personal stamp or impression through his entire body of work. Though this theory may initially seem flattering to directors—"we are each an artist making our statement" or "it is art because I, the artist, say it is"—it should be noted that here theorists would readily distinguish between directors based upon their ability.[23] Not all directors are worthy of consideration. In fact, there needs to be a significant body of work and then perhaps some time between the theorist and this body of work. What is more, this body of work must be judged overall as being very good. It is the critics and the theorists, not the directors themselves, who have the last word on who is and who is not an auteur.

Andrew Sarris posits three premises used to keep the Auteur theory from being abused:

1. To be an auteur, a director must display technical competence and flair for the cinema; to be great he must first at least be good at what matters at the most basic level of film production.

2. To be an auteur, a director must display a distinguishable personality and exhibit recurrent characteristics of style that serve as his signature.

3. To be an auteur, there must ultimately be a tension between the director and his material that results in an "interior meaning." This interior meaning is not so much

the director's worldview as it is his "soul," that is, "the intangible difference between one personality and another."[24]

This third point especially shows that the Auteur theory is not about directors who make what may be identified as "message films." A "message film" is a deliberate attempt to manipulate the viewer's beliefs and attitudes about a specific issue.[25] According to the Auteur theory, great directors simply make movies intended to entertain (the primary goal of a film) through telling a story in the medium of film. This special group of directors, however, exhibit work that is technically brilliant and marked by their unique personality while at the same time communicating also the director-as-author's unique understanding of reality. How this understanding then affects the understanding of the viewers would come about in a more subtle way than simply exposing the audience to some obvious message. And yet, if one takes this theory seriously, one would expect that the great films made by the great directors would have had (and continue to have) a profound effect upon the American viewers' understanding of reality and themselves in it.

As an example, Peter Wollen considers the work of American director Howard Hawks.[26] Wollen distinguishes two patterns in Hawks' overall body of work that present a great paradox. First, in his dramas and action films, Hawks depicts a "male-dominated world." In such stories he often focuses upon an elite group of male comrades who are men-of-action and who comprise a tight-knit group that others cannot easily access. This group may be involved in providing a service to greater society, yet they nevertheless remain distinct from it. A female character may with great difficulty and persistence break into this all-male group and then, after a prolonged courtship, become matched up (usually) with the leader of this group—but the primary relationships stressed at the surface level of the film are those between the male characters. In the world of Hawks' action dramas, men remain masters of all things—including nature, women, and children—and their most important bond is with one another.

In his comedic films, however, Hawks reverses the power relationships. In his comedies the main male character experiences a regression where he is no longer the master of all things. Some of these films then have a dominant female who hampers weaker men and/or pursues the male lead, often initially against his will. *Hawks' comedies, thus, are an inverse of the action dramas in the place and roles assigned to men.* Thus in his own expression evident in his overall body of work Hawks reveals some paradoxical tensions underlying reality, tensions having to do with the role and relationships of men and women.[27]

Perhaps these tensions could best be understood in light of theories associated with structuralism.[28] Underlying Hawks' entire body of work is the underlying fundamental binary opposition between male and female. In the action films the all-male community of heroes is portrayed as an ultimate reality. Such an all-male community may be necessary at times to help human society deal with threats to its stability. When a man is in such a community, he may revel in his autonomy, toughness, and power. And the men who risk their lives in such efforts would then appear heroic. But such a community could never procreate and produce the next generation. To procreate, the hero cannot remain in the all-male society, but must engage in a relationship with a woman. But in doing this he also risks losing his own mastery and autonomy both to her and then eventually to any children they produce. The tension is a part of the human experience and, what is more, it is frankly impossible to resolve this tension fully and completely in the lives of real men and women. Resolution on film—or here in an overall body of films—however, gives the viewer feelings of satisfaction. And so many viewers have resonated with the films of Howard Hawks because his films resonate with certain underlying realities of the general human condition.

Notice that there is not so much an explicit message that Hawks was communicating as there is an understanding of reality, especially the relationships between men and women, which he communicated in the stories he told through the medium of film. What is more, according to this structuralist understanding, Hawks' intentions were simply to make good movies; he himself did not have to be aware of what he was doing as he made these films. A key challenge to a theorist of film and a cultural observer, then, is to evaluate how this director may be reflecting an understanding of reality that is shared by him and his viewers and then—as an auteur—how he may have affected and influenced both the viewers of his films and also the filmmakers and films that come after him.

The Auteur theory may seem at odds with the Ideological approach, since the former argues that each director/author affects meaning in his film while the latter argues that such meaning is derived from the societal, cultural superstructure lying behind the film. But there can be interplay between these two theories. The Auteur theory has been understood in terms of structuralism: the best directors are those who are simply better at reflecting the binary oppositions underlying reality in their films.[29] What is more, some Ideologists will allow that the auteur may be good enough to actually critique (even if unintentionally and unknowingly) the main ideology and (perhaps even without trying) produce a film that may actually be subversive.[30]

The Ideological Theory of Film and Understanding the American Mind

Because the Ideological theory of film originated in the late 1960s, its (initial) focus has been upon films made before this time. Thus the film-making that came under consideration was especially those movies made during the classical age of Hollywood film production (1929–1967).[31] This time period overlaps also with the work of notable directors whose films cover this entire range of time, to include John Ford, Alfred Hitchcock, Frank Capra, Howard Hawks, and Billy Wilder. It was films of this era made by directors such as these that the Ideological theory would use to provide a lens by which to view "the American ideology." The point is made that it was in the classical period especially when most films were produced through the Hollywood studio system and when that studio system had economic control of the production and (until 1947) the distribution of films. Theorists following this approach claim they can detect an ideological framework underlying American cinema that reflects this economic reality.[32]

What is/was this ideology? Robin Wood identifies it as "the American capitalist ideology." It was the values and assumptions of the American capitalist system that were "so insistently embodied in and reinforced by the classical Hollywood cinema."[33] Wood offers the following list of components found in American films that demonstrate such values and assumptions:[34]

1. Capitalism: the right to ownership, private enterprise, personal initiative; the settling of the land.
2. The work ethic: honest toil is in and of itself morally admirable.
3. Marriage (legalized heterosexual marriage) and family: the homestead/house is built for the woman; the woman embodies civilization.
4. Nature as agrarian v. nature as wilderness: nature as agrarian denotes man's call to establish a Garden of Eden in virgin land; nature as wilderness denotes the need to civilize and subjugate.
5. Progress: technology and the city are good.
6. Pro-wealth: the allure of success and wealth.
7. Anti-wealth: the warning against success and wealth ("The Rosebud syndrome"); "money isn't everything; it corrupts."[35]

8. The American dream: America is the land where every one is or can be happy.

Out of this list then emerge the following two ideal figures or archetypes and their shadow counterparts:[36]

9. The ideal male: the virile, potent, untrammeled adventurer and man of action.
10. The ideal female: the wife and mother, perfect companion, endlessly dependable.
11. The counterpart to the ideal male: The settled husband and father, dependable but dull.
12. The counterpart to the ideal female: The erotic woman, fascinating but dangerous, liable to betray.[37]

Wood then notes that "[t]he most striking fact about this list is that it presents an ideology that, far from being monolithic, is *inherently* riddled with hopeless contradictions and irresolvable tensions."[38] If one wants to use film as a lens to detect and evaluate the American mind, the importance of this point made by Wood should not be underestimated: this American worldview is not one typified by unity and agreement in beliefs, ideas, assumptions, and experiences, but it is rather marked by contradiction and tension. There is an inherent tension between the allure of money and yet the warning against it and the idea that those without it are happier than those who have it. There is an inherent tension between the allure of nature in its wild and pristine state and yet the need to tame it by establishing farms, towns, and cities. There is inherent tension between the belief that progress is good and yet the idea that people were happier when life was simple. And there is especially an inherent tension between the ideal male and the ideal female: *As an ideal couple they are actually incompatible!* The ideal female, it seems, would be able to fulfill her role much more readily with the counterpart male—but, according to the formula, this would not be "ideal."

With this there is then also an inherent tension between the role of the ideal male—the free adventurer and man of action who most often figures as the main character—and the basic goal of settling down and bringing order to the wilderness: one would think that this "ideal man" would prefer the free and open wilderness to the encroachment of civilization with its rules. There could also be an inherent tension between the goals—establishing peaceful agrarian communities and/or cities—and the means—employing violence to subjugate Indians, criminals, or others who get in the way of progress. One other tension is that the villains most often display the characteristics of the ideal male (free men of action who do what they want) with the only difference being that the ideal man (eventually) sides with the order and civilization symbolized by the ideal woman.

Resolution of these tensions comes in the film usually when the ideal man does settle down with the ideal woman in the context of the narrative of the film. Such is often the conclusion of many westerns. Consider, for instance, *The Virginian* (1929) and *The Westerner* (1940) with Gary Cooper, and *Angel and the Badman* (1947) and *Hondo* (1953) with John Wayne. It is notable that in the two Gary Cooper films the hero must also be involved in the death of a man who was once his friend. In both cases the friend is a man who prefers the freedom of the wilderness to the coming order of civilization, and this same freedom is what the main character is also depicted as possessing, but then giving up. In choosing to kill his friend, the ideal male has chosen the ideal female over the chaos and freedom represented by his friend—a freedom he, the ideal male, also once possessed and a freedom that just happens to be one important characteristic that makes this character ideal. The implication is that in settling down, *that same freedom is now given up by the ideal male*. The viewer, however, does not see the implications of this final act of the ideal male relinquishing his freedom to marry and settle down as the film ends before these are shown.

This relinquishing of former freedom is made very plain in the Wayne film *Angel and the Badman*. In this film the ideal male (played by Wayne) is an outlaw. He falls in love with the ideal female, a woman who is the member of a Quaker community and thus devoted to nonviolence. The woman's Quaker father, a potential suitor, and other male members of the Quaker community are all examples of the shadow counterpart to the ideal male. In the story the ideal male wavers between keeping his autonomy and settling down with the woman whom he now loves. As one would expect, in the end he chooses to give up his freedom. But not only does he relinquish his freedom, in the climax of the film he also gives up his revolver—*and he literally hands it over to the ideal female*. This gun is used symbolically throughout this film to mark this man for what he is—a "badman," a self-reliant, independent warrior who is at odds with civilization. To give up this tool seems suicidal in the film, for this act renders him vulnerable to his enemies. But he refuses to fight anymore if that is what the female wants. Instead of remaining a free outlaw, he will become a farmer—the occupation of the woman's father and most of the other counterparts in this film.

But the story ends before the viewer gets to see what this would look like. The ideal male and female ride off together happily into the sunset, but the audience is not privy to the next morning when this man must rise and begin his new and less exciting life as a farmer. It is at this same point that similar films end, and the viewer rarely gets to see what it looks like when the very next day the ideal male must now begin to resemble the counterpart male in a less free, less autonomous state of existence.[39]

What is demonstrated by this analysis of the ideology behind films of the classical era of Hollywood film production? *One important point is that there was/is not some monolithic ideology that would comprise the "American mind."* Rather, there are tensions underlying this American ideology. In film these tensions are often resolved, but in the real world of American life these tensions are not so easily resolved. Some of these tensions speak to concerns that are universal to humanity, and thus not uniquely American. This would include the concern that men and women should come together for marriage and procreation, that this is fundamental to the building of human communities, but that in doing this there must be compromise—actually, on the part of both men and women. Such compromise is not always readily achieved in reality, but people find satisfaction in finding it resolved in a narrative.

But there are also tensions that one could argue are more unique to the American experience. One such tension would be between the belief that capitalism is good and the acknowledgment that capitalism has a dark side in fostering greed and exploitation. Another such tension would be between the belief that progress is good and the acknowledgement that life was better when it was simpler.[40] Another tension would be between the belief that pristine nature is good and the belief that it must be tamed and populated in such a way that its pristine state is lost. One other such tension would be between the belief that the establishment of the American nation has been basically a good thing for universal mankind—now the immigrants come here for a better life—and yet the acknowledgement that this nation was established in part through violence visited upon Native Americans and others. American films of this era reflect these tensions in the narratives they tell. In these narratives on film the tensions may often be resolved. In reality, however, they remain unresolved—and it is in reality that the viewers of film must ultimately live.

The Archetypes

It is worth discussing further the identification of the archetypes and the counterparts to these archetypes. The archetypical figure of that time was the independent, individualist male—a free man who is not beholden to anyone. This man is tough, virile, and dangerous, yet he is also heroic and will do the right thing—and this in the end distinguishes him from the villains who, interestingly, share some or many of his same characteristics. This archetypical figure is a fighter and a winner. According to the ideology, civilization and order—and the capitalist structure—could not exist or advance without men like this. He is the ideal man every woman should want. If one considers here the psychoanalytical assumptions underlying the Ideological approach, then he is also the ideal man every man should want to become. The power of film is such that it would lead the viewers—at least the male audience in this era—to identify themselves with this figure and then, in a sense, to become this character while watching a film. Given this archetype, it may be seen how this character both reflects and reinforces many values that mark Americans and their culture—values such as individual freedom, autonomy, and independence.

On the other hand, the counterparts to this archetypical male—the loyal but boring husband/father—are cast as somehow less ideal. In film the counterpart may fill the role of the archetype's sidekick, the father or brother or rival suitor of the ideal woman, the passive farmer or laborer who is victimized and in need of being rescued or avenged, usually the non-white male characters (at least those who are not villains), and so on. If the Ideological approach is correct, then the viewer would not identify as strongly with such characters. One could then guess at the possible tensions this paradox could create in the mind of the viewer who happens to be an American male: this viewer is led to identify with the free and independent archetype, but not with this archetype's shadow counterpart. But this same viewer is to see as part of the ideal this man's need to settle down and marry—and thus become the counterpart.

Yet which character in reality would make the better husband, father, citizen, neighbor, or, we might add, Christian believer—the archetype or its counterpart? In film it is the former—though in film the story often ends before the audience gets to see what it looks like when this character will relinquish his freedom to settle down. In reality the ideal woman might be better off marrying the counterpart to the archetype. Yet at the same time viewers are never to identify with this counterpart. The ideal male is thus tasked to fulfill a role he is not really suited for; the counterpart who is best suited for that role is, nevertheless, not seen as ideal. Tensions and contradictions that may be resolved in film remain unresolved in reality.

There are then several questions that emerge when considering this: can the ideal male truly settle down without giving up the characteristics that make him ideal—and if not, why would he want to settle down? How can society exist without the dependable men who give up independence and individuality, at least to some extent, in order to devote themselves to a wife and children—and hence to greater society itself? What does it say when the archetype is pictured as the ideal, but the counterpart is not?

Perhaps in the narrative in the film there is resolution when the ideal couple finally settles down and the ideal male compromises his autonomy for the sake of marriage, family, and society. Nevertheless, as mentioned above, in the film one rarely sees how this compromise works itself out: the hero is protected from the viewers having to see his compromise and instead he remains in their mind more or less still in his ideal, independent, individualistic, autonomous state. Is this depiction of the archetypical figure a true reflection of American beliefs and values? How has it shaped an American worldview? Has such a depiction shaped American audiences—especially American males—and their understanding of reality and their place in it? Does this image still endure in film? Should this archetype be critiqued? How should such a critique be offered?

One other issue emerges, an issue which film theorists have noted: It should seem clear that this system is very much focused upon the centrality, not just of the male, but of the dominant white male who is/was at the top of the social order. A partial response to this "heterosexual-white-male-centered ideology" has been either (1) to offer a deconstructive viewing of classic films by identifying with the point of view of other characters or (2) to make new films that substitute some character other than a heterosexual white male in the place of the archetype, while then stressing the heterosexual white male's role instead as being that of villain or shadow. Do these approaches offer a proper critique and response to the ideology promoting this archetype?

Finally, there is one further issue of concern for Christian believers: do the attitudes and ideals underlying the American ideology as exemplified by the American archetypical hero reflect in any way "the mind of Christ"? If one takes the Ideological approach seriously, any critique of the "archetype" would also be a critique of the American culture that produced films with such archetypes. According to some theorists who use the Ideological approach, there was one film genre that emerged in the classical era that provides a critique of the American ideology by showing a stark photonegative of the American story. Other theorists who blend the Ideological approach with that of the Auteur theory find that critiques of the archetype and the ideology this character represents were actually made in film during this very same classical era. Such "critiques" will be considered next.

Critique of the American Ideology and the Archetypical Figure

Critique of what Wood calls "the American capitalist ideology" would come from within the system of filmmaking itself during the classical era. (Note that such critique could be explained from the very tensions underlying the American reality.) First, in the aftermath of World War II and then in the emerging Cold War era, a film genre emerged that has since been interpreted as a critique of the ideology reflected in the major studio films of the first phase of the classical period (1929–1948). This genre is now known commonly as *film noir*. These films tended to be dark—not only thematically, but also in the actual lighting of the frames.[41] In *film noir* the American dream has instead become an American nightmare, the old optimism replaced with a new pessimism. The main character is often the archetype identified by Wood—an independent, autonomous, and individualistic male—but in these films his conflict is not to establish a greater good, but often the acquisition of money and power or sometimes simply his own survival. Such films are said, in part, to be a reflection of a negative mood experienced by many in the post-War period. *Film noir* has been interpreted as one critique of the American ideology evident in the studio productions in that it provides a photonegative reflection of the ideal American world in which everything is turned around and things are no longer ideal.[42]

The ideology of the major studio films of the classical period would also later undergo a critique by certain films made by directors of the post-classical or "New Hollywood" period (1967–1980). Several notable films of this era would offer a critical look at the capitalistic system and the American dream. Such films would include *The Graduate* (1967), *Bonnie and Clyde* (1967), *Midnight Cowboy* (1969), *The Wild Bunch* (1969), *The Godfather* parts 1 (1972) and 2 (1974), and *Taxi Driver* (1976). In offering this critique of the ideology, each film would also offer a different take on and portrayal of the archetypical figure.

But several notable critiques of this ideology may be detected during the classical period itself. I will discuss two such critiques, one offered by director/auteur John Ford in *The Searchers* (1956) and one offered by director/auteur Frank Capra in *It's a Wonderful Life* (1946).

The American Archetype Critiqued by an Auteur: John Ford and *The Searchers*

The Searchers is a western film that tells the story of the five-year quest of its main character, Ethan Edwards, to recover his niece who was kidnapped by the Comanche Indians. Edwards is played by actor John Wayne. This casting becomes key in that Wayne, more than any other American actor, has been said to embody the archetype of the rugged, adventurous, independent, individualistic, autonomous man of action in American cinema. In this film the archetype is played by an iconic actor who in the American culture is one who is most closely identified with that archetype.

The film begins in such a way as to highlight that the character of Ethan Edwards is the archetype: a woman, Edwards' sister-in-law, opens the door of her home—the home being the symbol of order and civilization—to see Edwards alone and riding a horse out from the wilderness. Edwards is the archetype, the ideal male. This woman—a wife, mother, and keeper of the home—is the ideal female. In fact, it soon becomes apparent that she and Edwards are in love with one another. And yet she is not married to Edwards, but to his brother. It is soon apparent also that this other man, Edwards' brother, is one who is clearly the counterpart to the archetype—the dependable but boring male. Another story might tell of the brother's death and so the need for Edwards to assume the role of husband and father in relation to his sister-in-law and her children. In this way the goal of the ideal male and female coming together would be fulfilled.

In this story, however, Edwards' brother and his sister-in-law, along with his nephew and one niece, are soon killed in a Comanche raid. Edwards' younger niece, Debbie, has been captured and taken to live with the Comanche. The goal of this story now is the recovery of Edwards' niece. Edwards is joined in this quest by his brother's adopted son, the part-Indian Martin Pawley (played by Jeffrey Hunter). *What is impossible at this point, however, is that the ideal male (Ethan Edwards) and the ideal female (his sister-in-law) can come together*. This film has now a different goal.

That Ethan Edwards is the archetype remains clear throughout the remainder of this film, and this is evident especially in the film's depiction of the other male characters. Compared with Edwards, nearly every other male character in this film comes off as just another example of a "less-than-ideal" counterpart male. Edwards' character mocks these other males, holds them in disdain and contempt, and consistently gets the better of them. This is true also in Edwards' relationship with his adopted nephew, Martin Pawley. Martin shares some of Edwards' traits—somewhat wild and untamed. He too is introduced in the film riding his horse out from the wilderness alone. He too could be something of an outsider. Yet Martin has an established place in his adopted parents' home. And even though Martin joins Edwards in this quest to recover Debbie, his character never seems to achieve Edwards' level of rugged independence or his mastery over others. Edwards will mock Martin, order him about, recklessly endanger his life, and so on. In fact, the only character who mirrors Edwards to any degree in this film is his Comanche counterpart, the chief Scar who organized the raid on the homestead of Edwards' brother. Both men are fueled by racial hatred and old grievances. And so hero and villain are practically mirror-images of one another.

Given the manner in which Ethan Edwards is portrayed, an interesting experience takes place after repeated viewings of this film. It is clear from the opening scene that his character is the archetype. Nevertheless, the audience is forced to view Ethan Edwards as an increasingly less than ideal character. He instead emerges as a rather ambivalent character. First, there is the fact made clear at the beginning of the film that he is the ideal male, but, for whatever reason, he has failed to settle down with the ideal female and this in spite of the fact that they obviously love one another. Then there are other things that occur in the narrative: Edwards refuses to linger too long at the funeral of his family, as if this were a waste of his time. He is depicted shooting out the eyes of a dead Comanche warrior to ensure this man's being disabled in (his own view of) the afterlife. He shoots fleeing Comanche Indians in the back while they are in retreat. Such actions as these result in moral outrage from the other "white male" characters (and the audience?), but Edwards remains unmoved. Then, as the film proceeds, he constantly belittles and treats the likeable Martin with contempt. Later, in a seemingly crazed fit, he guns down buffalo simply to deny food to the Comanche—victimizing, among others, innocent Comanche women and children. And finally, most disturbing of all, given the nature of his quest, he becomes determined to kill Debbie instead of rescuing her once he learns that she has become one of Scar's wives. The foil to Edwards throughout the entire narrative is the ever dependable and faithful, but always less individualistic, independent, and masterful Martin.

When the film reaches its climax, it is not Edwards, surprisingly, who proves the hero in any traditional understanding of the hero's role. The Comanche tribe is routed in an attack of cavalry and Texas Rangers led by the Preacher (Ward Bond), and all Edwards does is take part in this battle. In the meantime, Martin risks his life by sneaking into the Comanche camp by night ahead of time to rescue Debbie on his own; while rescuing Debbie, Martin is forced to kill Scar. Thus there is nothing for Edwards to do in the end but scalp Scar's dead body. In the final action, in fact, the viewer does not see Edwards do anything other than this one jarring act. It is not even shown that he kills any Comanche in this fight. What is more, it appears as if Edwards is driven more by a desire to avenge his sister-in-law's death than by any more noble goals.

The film's true climax comes when Edwards finally has a chance to fulfill his desire to kill his niece. She flees from him while Martin chases him from behind. But when he reaches his niece, Edwards suddenly relents and embraces her instead of killing her. It is not really explained why he does this; he just does. Debbie is then brought to live with the Jorgensens—a family of Swedish settlers and friends of Edwards' deceased brother. Martin unites with the Jorgensens' daughter, his love interest throughout the film, whom he now plans to marry. The closing scene recalls the opening scene of the film. The viewer looks from the Jorgensen homestead out onto the wilderness. Lucy, Martin, and various other characters enter into the Jorgensen household in groups. But Ethan Edwards himself does not enter the house even as he watches the others do so. This is important, for the homestead, again, is the symbol of family, order, and civilization. Even the part-Indian Martin and Indian-dressed Debbie are allowed to enter. But the archetype is not allowed. He is left outside in the wilderness. The door of the home closes on Edwards as he is still outside, walking away back toward the wilderness. He will have no part in the future.

Whether or not he intended this, John Ford offers what amounts to a stunning critique and rejection of the American archetypical figure in *The Searchers*. That this figure is played by John Wayne—the archetypical actor who is best known for playing the archetypical American hero—makes this critique all the more stunning. Upon subsequent viewings, Wayne's character cannot, in fact, be interpreted as anything heroic or admirable, even though he is the archetype. Ethan Edwards actually accomplishes nothing by his five-year search. Although he does eventually locate Debbie, he cannot rescue her when he first finds her. And by this time, in fact, his motives have changed: he is instead determined to murder her because she has been married to a "Comanche buck." In the end it is the character of Martin Pawley who rescues Debbie and avenges the death of his adopted parents (though this revenge is not his intention). All there is for the archetype to do in the end is scalp the dead body of his enemy and then decide not to carry out his cruel intentions toward his niece.[43] Strangely, then, if there is a hero in this film, it would seem to be Martin Pawley, not Ethan Edwards.

And yet Martin is never allowed to become the archetype. He remains the dependable, boring, moralistic, sometimes dopey sidekick throughout most of the film. Yet, with subsequent viewings of this film, as the viewer is led to be repulsed more and more by the character of Ethan Edwards, Martin Pawley naturally replaces Ethan as the one with whom the viewer must identify. And so the ideal is no longer the rugged individualist, but the dependable man who has ties to a moral code and to other people. Martin also sacrifices five years of his life to find Debbie—though strangely nothing was made of this in either the film's trailer or in the film's main theme which both focus instead upon the wandering of Ethan Edwards. Yet unlike Edwards, Martin actually does have better things to be doing during the time of this quest: he can marry the Jorgensen girl. He instead sacrifices his personal happiness and nearly gives up any potential future with his love interest for the sake of his adopted sister. Martin later risks his own life to rescue his sister. And he is the only one willing to confront

Edwards in the matter of his desire to kill Debbie—the sidekick standing up to the archetype.

When male and female do come together in this film, it is Martin—the still less-than-ideal man—who will finally marry the Jorgensen girl—who has become the ideal woman by this point in the film. The archetype does not settle down, but is shut out in the wilderness. Instead, it is the counterpart who gets the woman. The male viewer of *The Searchers* may feel the tension between remaining outside with Ethan Edwards—free and autonomous, but alone—or entering the house with Martin and the others—less autonomous and tied down to other people, yet still a part of the future. It seems Ford's film would move the viewer to choose the latter option and leave the archetype in the wilderness of past history. In what is considered by many his greatest film, Ford portrays the archetype as a man who cannot be a part of the home, who cannot settle down with the female archetype, who is left in the dustbin of the American frontier—which, of course, is now closed. The stark finale leaves this character standing alone outside and shut out from human companionship, and the male viewer is perhaps left with the impression that to be like this man is to face this same fate. In subsequent viewings a new ideal character emerges, not the archetype, but the counterpart, not Ethan Edwards, but Martin Pawley.

The American Ideology Critiqued by an Auteur: Frank Capra and *It's a Wonderful Life*

It can be argued *It's a Wonderful Life* has emerged as the most enduring film directed by Frank Capra.[44] Robin Wood notes, however, that this film has perhaps some of the most negative and subversive elements of any Capra film.[45] The main character, George Bailey, is a man who spends most of this film wanting to be more like the American archetypical figure—a free and traveling adventurer, an independent individualist with no ties to anyone, even a successful industrialist and capitalist. Strange, but in this movie Bailey wants to be more like the film's villain, Mr. Potter. But George is instead forced to live as the counterpart to the archetype—the faithful and dependable husband, father, and neighbor. The fact that this character is played by actor James Stewart is also key, for Stewart more than any other American actor is said to have embodied the character of the regular, dependable, "aw shucks" American male (though Stewart too would play many archetype roles).

But Stewart's Bailey is actually played against type: he does not spend most of this film content with or feeling ennobled by the ideals that characterize his life—the ideals of self-giving and sacrifice in service to family and neighbor—the very ideals that in this story motivate the forces of heaven itself to save him from suicide. Instead George Bailey is portrayed as one who is bitter about missed opportunities to escape his hometown of Bedford Falls, first to travel the world, then to attend college or work in the city, and then finally to fight in World War II. No matter what the situation, there is a reason George Bailey cannot leave Bedford Falls. He acts as one who is stuck in a rut, and he is deeply embittered by this life he did not want but has been forced to live. And so when things go wrong, his final desire is to kill himself, motivated by the thought that he is "worth more dead than alive."

But then, in an attempt to keep him from committing suicide, George is offered an ultimate chance to be what he has always wanted to be—to be the archetype, completely free and autonomous, with absolutely no ties to anyone or anything. This is what it means if he gets to live as if he had never been born. In the alternate universe that George is allowed to view he is, in fact, finally a free and independent man. But what he sees is not the ideal American life, but the *film noir* photonegative version of this life. The happy town of Bedford Falls is now a dark place called Pottersville. The main street of this town is littered with bars, pawn shops, and strip joints rather than small shops and businesses. Each and every one of his family, friends, and neighbors is now either dead or leading a miserable, pointless existence. Thus the price of George's wish to be what one could call the ultimate incarnation of the archetype—one who is alive, yet who does not exist and so has no ties to anyone, the ultimate free and autonomous agent—would mean ultimate misery for his town and everyone he knows. The happy if less-than-ideal community of Bedford Falls is the result of George Bailey's self-sacrifice and service to his neighbor, and thus of his refusal to become the archetype. Without this service, there would be hell on earth. In Capra's film both views of reality are possible—the ideal America or the *film noirish* photonegative. It all depends upon the choices that a man like George Bailey would make. He could be the archetype, but if he chooses this for himself, the *film noir* reality would result.

Robin Wood notes this tension in *It's a Wonderful Life*:

> The film recognizes explicitly that behind every Bedford Falls lurks a Pottersville, and implicitly that within every George Bailey lurks an Ethan Edwards of *The Searchers*. Potter, tempting George, is given the devil's insight into his suppressed dreams. His remark, "You once called me a warped, frustrated old man—now you're a warped, frustrated *young* man," is amply supported by the evidence the film supplies.[46]

Woods, apparently operating from a structuralist view, argues that Bailey is trapped in Bedford Falls by the women in the film, both his mother and his wife Mary—each who embodies the archetype of "the ideal woman."[47] Wood's critique, however, fails to note that when the character of George Bailey first opts to remain in Bedford Falls, it is because of his ideals, not a female character. In the film George is first portrayed as a boy who seems the archetype—dynamic, independent, fun-loving, a leader among the other boys. His father, on the other hand, is the longsuffering, dependable counterpart to the archetype—a hard-working man who struggles for the sake of his neighbors to maintain his business, the Bailey Building and Loan, and uncomplainingly endures the harassment of the greedy and power-hungry Mr. Potter. When George is grown and plans to leave Bedford Falls, his father suddenly dies. The only way to keep his father's work alive is for him to stay, for without the Building and Loan the common citizens of Bedford Falls would have no option but "to crawl to Potter." George could leave, but chooses to stay because his neighbors need for him to stay. By staying and continuing his father's work, George gives up his dreams, but also helps his neighbors live a better life.

It is only when George has his second chance to leave, but again declines, this time for the sake of his younger brother's future marriage and career, that he is drawn to seek marriage with Mary. And so it is not so much female wiles but George's own tendency to put the needs of others before himself that keeps him trapped in Bedford Falls and thus keeps him from becoming an Ethan Edwards—a free man beholden to no one. It is rather Mr. Potter who appears more the archetype—independent, autonomous, powerful. But Potter is also crippled and embittered, and the only way he can beat George is ultimately by stealing from him. Yet Potter is correct in his assessment of George: George is also embittered, spending most of the film unhappy and self-absorbed. But this is because as a character he has not yet been shown that the ideals he actually longs after—those of the archetype—are secondary to the higher ideal he exhibits through loving his neighbors. At the end of the film, however, after the prayers of his family and friends muster the forces of heaven itself to save his life, George Bailey is reconciled to his calling in life, and then is noted to be "the richest man in town."

Capra is said to have remarked once that a key theme of his films was embodied in the second of the great commandments: "Love Thy Neighbor."[48] In his most enduring work Capra perhaps shows that the American archetypical hero—that of the autonomous individualist—exhibits values that would be antithetical to the keeping of this commandment. At the same time Capra perhaps also warns against the dangers of "unfeeling capitalism," a system where greed and selfishness overshadow love and concern for the welfare of others.[49] In this Capra offers a critique to aspects of the system and its narrative archetype. Not only this, but in this film he offers a different kind of hero: George Bailey is not the autonomous, individualist loner who lives for himself—although this is what he wants for himself—but he is in the end a faithful son, brother, husband, father, friend, and neighbor, one who continuously puts the interests of others ahead of his own. George Bailey thus stands in stark contrast with Ethan Edwards as to what would embody "the ideal American male."

Some Reflections: The American Mind and the Mind of Christ

When considering what the Ideological approach to film criticism would label "the American capitalist ideology," the Christian church could find certain beliefs, attitudes, values, and ideas in this system which it could affirm. The central role of marriage and family in human life, the value of hard work to make one's living, the belief that criminal deviancy is morally evil and worthy of punishment, that government exists to establish order that is beneficial to its citizens[50]—these are good things a Lutheran might associate with the First Article and thus determine to be gifts to us and all people from God the Father, our Creator. The coming together of man and woman for marriage as the goal of many such films perhaps continues to mirror the story of the first man and woman in Eden as told in Genesis 2. Since marriage is one basic feature of human existence, this remains a popular theme and goal in narratives; again, a Christian can respect this as one aspect of our created existence. That the ideal male in American films of the classical era usually does, in fact, give up his freedom for the sake of marriage and family can be argued to affirm this basic element of God's created order.

When considering these same values that the church may openly affirm, the observer should nevertheless be aware of how these values in American films may both reflect and *affirm a uniquely American view* of these values in this American context. In this reflection the values may be universal to created human existence, but their expression is contextual to the American way of living out these values. Though the expression of these values may be a good thing, the observer should be aware of certain American ways of expressing them that may not be a feature in other cultures. For example, in American cinema of the classical era, the ideal family was often shown as consisting of a nuclear family—husband, wife, and children—living together in one house isolated even from other family members; this is not necessarily how humanity has always experienced family and so it is not necessarily "better" than other expressions, such as an extended family living together. Films of this era, however, could give the impression not only that family is good, but that the American nuclear family is the best way for this ideal to be realized.

Then, if one were to understand things more in light of the Ideological approach, the observer may also want to be aware of how the expression of these values in film may be used not only to foster these same values among viewers of film (which some might say is a good thing), but also to support certain power structures in our society. In this, film may not only promote certain values or expressions, but at the same time it could suppress other values or expressions. For example, to affirm the ideal family as a nuclear family living together could at the same time amount to the suppression of the extended family existence. This is evident in films where members of the nuclear family living together are portrayed as modern, civilized, and sophisticated where members of extended families living together are portrayed as less civilized and sophisticated, and perhaps even primitive or savage. In this scheme the nuclear family living together is comprised of people who are "normal Americans" while the extended family living together typifies the life-style of Native Americans, immigrants (usually southern European, Latin American, or Asian), or rural Americans of the American South or West in the post-frontier era. Such depictions make and reinforce a value judgment on what is entailed in the ideal family, showing one system as ideal and others as less than ideal. With this the ideologist might argue such films promote a power structure that benefits old stock Americans who live in town and city over Native Americans, recent immigrants, and Americans who continue to live in rural areas.

Next, when considering the *experiences* that lay at the heart of "the American capitalist ideology" in the films of this era and how these are evaluated, perhaps some very interesting debate may arise among observers, debate that may not be so easily resolved. Some of the past American experiences that can be seen to underlie films of the classical era would include this nation's original struggle for independence from Great Britain, the westward movement across the continent in its various stages and the frontier existence in the West, and industrialization and the advance of technology. Important American experiences that then took place contemporaneous with the classical era and which may also be seen underlying many films of this time would be the Great Depression, the American participation in World War II, the emergence of the Cold War, and, perhaps also, the nascent Civil Rights Movement.

Note that these experiences are simply a part of the American story. It is how they are understood in film that would give rise to debate: how should the church evaluate the understanding of these experiences in film? Was the War of Independence a just action which led to the founding of the best and freest nation in human history? Or was it a violation of the fourth commandment, especially when understood from our Lutheran perspective? Does the westward movement represent the advance of human progress and a partial fulfillment of God's directive to humankind in Genesis 1 as well as his destiny for the United States? Or was it instead a criminal violation of the rights of Native Americans and Hispanics who were here first as well as an environmental disaster with the destruction of pristine nature? Does industrialization represent the advance of human progress? Or did it lead to the de-valuing of human existence, further destruction of the environment, and our enslavement to technology? Could there be "both-and" and "yes-and-no" answers to many of these questions?

According to an understanding influenced by the Ideological approach, films of the classical era probably would have tended to affirm the basic goodness of these experiences—the War of Independence, the westward expansion, industrialization—as it was necessary to do this in order to support the capitalist system of twentieth-century America. But the fact that this was not always the response in cinema shows that American society was to some degree aware of the other side of these issues. If aware of what is going on in film, the Christian Church might offer fresh evaluations of these values and experiences that underlie the American self-understanding. I mention such issues not to provide a definitive answer to any of these questions, but simply to raise awareness of how the experiences reflected in American film could be evaluated. Notice how Wood's analysis of the ideology remains true in evaluating the American mind: Even as the ideology itself is riddled with contradictions, there also is no monolithic response that can be offered. There is much that can be affirmed by the Church and much that must be questioned and perhaps rejected. Tension remains.

The Mind of the Archetype and the Mind of Christ

I will now consider the archetypes of American film—the ideal American male and female—in terms of what would constitute "the ideal Christian person." As mentioned above, that the ideal male character most often compromises his freedom to settle down and marry could be interpreted as a good thing. However, as also mentioned above, most often the implications of what this means for this character's "ideal status" is suspended from the narrative—and this becomes problematic for the viewers.

This last point is key: what makes the ideal male ideal is his freedom, independence, autonomy, and mastery over others.[51] (Note how some of these values can be traced directly or indirectly to our nation's basic understanding of itself as the nation that prizes individual liberty and freedom; perhaps the ideal male's mastery over others is one trait out of synch with these basic American ideals.) In the classic American film, when the ideal male settles down with the ideal female, he will give up these traits that make him ideal and will, in effect, soon become his own shadow counterpart. *The audience, however, never gets to see what this will be like as the movie ends at just this point.* Thus the ideal male is in a sense protected from actually losing the traits that make him ideal. From the perspective of the audience he remains in his ideal state. Again, resolution on film may provide satisfaction to the audience. In reality the viewer of such films—especially the American male viewer—is left to deal with a tension that is not so easily resolved: he is to understand that certain ideals embody "the ideal male"—values such as freedom, independence, autonomy, and mastery over others. At the same time, the projected goal is the establishment of marriage and family, goals which will call him to relinquish at least to a certain degree those things that would make him ideal. In the real world outside of the world of the film, tension remains.

How should the church critique this portrayal of the American archetype—"the ideal American"? If this archetype shows certain beliefs, knowledge, attitudes, ideas, and experiences that comprise the American mind, how should the church evaluate these? To answer we may consider these questions: what beliefs, knowledge, attitudes, ideas, and experiences would comprise the ideal Christian? If this archetype gives insight into "the American mind," how does this compare with "the mind of Christ"?

To discuss "the mind of Christ," I will use the passage in Philippians 2:5: Here the Apostle Paul exhorts, "Let this mind be in you, which was also in Christ Jesus."[52] This exhortation of the Apostle to the Christians at Philippi is part of the larger paraenesis section of Philippians 1:27–2:18,[53] but is especially noted for introducing the great Christological hymn of Philippians 2:6-11 which describes Jesus' humiliation and exaltation. The exhortation of 2:5 is then often read in light of that hymn. What does it mean to have "the mind of Christ Jesus"? In relationship to others (especially in the context of other believers) one would show this same humility, this same self-giving, sacrificial attitude as exemplified by Jesus—and then leave it to God to do any subsequent lifting up.[54]

Yet the exhortation of Philippians 2:5 should perhaps also be read in light of the exhortations that immediately precede it in 2:2-4: "Fulfill ye my joy, that ye be likeminded, having the same love, *being* of one accord, of one mind. *Let* nothing *be done* through strife or vainglory; but in lowliness of mind let each esteem others better than themselves. Look not every man on his own things, but every man also on the things of others" (Philippians 2:2-4). The Christological hymn follows this entire passage, not just 2:5. The exhortation and hymn in 2:5-11 provide both example and basis for the instruction of 2:1-4.[55]

Jesus did not give himself in humble self-sacrifice—ultimately even unto death by crucifixion—merely for the sake of doing it. He did this in humble service for these Christians whom Paul is addressing, to save them and to begin that good work in them that will be made complete on the last day (Philippians 1:6). And so they are exhorted in turn to live for the sake of one another. The exhortation of Philippians 2:5, then, should be read in light of both the exhortations that precede it and the Christological hymn that follows. If there is a "mind of Christ" to be found in Philippians 2, an attitude that he exemplifies and that his church is called to have as well, it is found in the exhortation to have this same mind or attitude—for each Christian not to act in selfishness, not to look out only for oneself, but to live in self-sacrificial humility and to consider the interests of others before oneself. This is outlined in Philippians 2:1–4.

For a Christian who is called to live and confess this faith in the context of the United States in the twenty-first century, any discussion of "the American mind" would have to consider also this "mind of Christ" as exemplified in Philippians 2 (and elsewhere in Scripture). We share common *beliefs, knowledge, and experience* with the Christians of Philippi who were addressed by Paul. We too were saved by Jesus Christ. Our Lord also put our interests ahead of his own in his humiliation and death upon the cross. Jesus began this good work in us which will be made perfect on the last day. We too know, believe, and confess Jesus as Lord. The paraenesis in Philippians 2 applies also to us. One means, then, to critique the American mind and its beliefs, knowledge, attitudes, ideas, and experiences would be the way in which we as Christians are called to faith and new life in Jesus. How is a Christian in America to evaluate the beliefs, attitudes, ideas, and experiences that make up the American mind in light of the exhortation to live as instructed in a passage such as Philippians 2:5—the admonition to have the same belief and attitude that Jesus had? Do the American archetypes show forth this same mind that we find also in Christ Jesus?

Perhaps this could be said of the ideal woman: her life is lived for others—husband and children—though the goal is specifically to establish house, family, and society. Such probably could not be said for the ideal male, however. Though this male will ultimately do the right thing and prove himself heroic in service to others, his own independence, individualism, autonomy, and, ultimately, high sense of himself could seem to negate any inclination that he would give himself in sacrifice and service to others. It is really more the counterpart male who resembles these attitudes of living for others, showing humility, not seeking himself, and so on. Such a person as this, however sympathetic he may be to the audience—and he may often not be so sympathetic—is simply not the ideal. The Ideological approach thus may very well show that the reflection of what constitutes "the ideal man" in Hollywood film of the classical era is to various degrees at odds with what constitutes the ideal person in the exhortation of the Apostle Paul.

Christian pastors in this American context should be aware of the role cinema has been playing in popular culture and thus of these archetypes that typify what constitutes "the ideal male and female" in this American context. With this the pastor should be aware of the tension that what is easily resolved in American cinema is not so easily resolved in real life. Thus to exhort a congregation of Jesus' disciples who also happen to be Americans—perhaps in particular the men of this congregation—a pastor should be aware of the tension between what Paul in Philippians 2 describes as the ideal man, namely Jesus himself, and what American popular culture through the medium of cinema portrays as the ideal man. To the extent that the archetypical male especially vies with the New Testament exhortation of the Christian life, the pastor would call upon his people to confess and live their Christian faith in ways that would speak against such an ideal based upon being a person who is autonomous, free, independent, individualistic, master of others, and so on. In Jesus Christ our Savior and Lord we have a new ideal person and one which challenges the ideals of our contemporary culture.

At the same time, Christians could greatly appreciate and be taught by those films that provide helpful critiques of this "American ideology" and its archetypes. As demonstrated in this paper, two of the greatest American films made by two of the greatest American directors offer such critiques. It is not that there are any overtly Christian themes in John Ford's *The Searchers* or in Frank Capra's *It's a Wonderful Life* (though some may try to argue this of the latter film). Rather, these two great directors both hold up the archetype in a very realistic and stark contrast against type; both also offer a more compelling and attractive portrayal of what typically would be the counterpart to the archetype. Ethan Edwards in *The Searchers* is from start to finish a man who is alone and who has no place in the home, and by the end of the film he is not even the hero; Martin Pawley, the counterpart, both fulfills the hero's role in this film and then settles down with the ideal female. In *It's a Wonderful Life*, George Bailey's unfulfilled longing to be the archetype is answered by the revelation that it is by being the counterpart to this archetype—the boring but dependable family man and neighbor—that he has been fulfilling the hero's role in society all along.

In what is arguably Ford's greatest film, the American archetype is shown to be what such a character in the real world would actually be: an antisocial discontent who has no place in the future. In what is arguably Capra's greatest film a new example is offered of what makes "the ideal American," a character which also perhaps ranks as one of few such characters in American film to exemplify almost fully the very pattern of living exhorted by Paul in Philippians 2. Christians can knowingly appreciate these and other American films in the way they can aid the church in speaking sometimes with, and sometimes against, the values of the surrounding culture in this American context in which we are called to confess and live out our Christian faith.

Endnotes

1 See Robyn Karney, *Chronicle of the Cinema: 100 Years of the Movies* (New York: DK Publishing, 1997), 12–13, W. Barnes Tatum, *Jesus at the Movies: A Guide to the First Hundred Years* (Santa Rosa: Polebridge Press, 1997), 1–2, and Toby Miller, "Hollywood and the World," in *The Oxford Guide to Film Studies*, edited by John Hill and Pamela Church Gibson (New York: Oxford University Press, 1998), 371–379.

2 It is from the 1920s on that American filmmaking took the lead on the world stage in pioneering innovative technology and new approaches to filmmaking. Before this the Europeans—and most especially the French—were the pioneers. See Karney, 12–13 and Miller, 371–372.

3 In this discussion one could also consider the influence of English-language films made by producers and directors of Great Britain and other Commonwealth nations. Such films have often used American actors, have been played in American theatres and thus watched by American audiences, have been nominated for and have won Academy Awards, and continue to be watched by American audiences via television, VCR, and DVD. Thus in the popular mind many such films may appear indistinguishable from American films. (The category for "Best Foreign Film" in the Academy Awards usually signifies "a non-English language film.") Consider, for instance, David Lean's *The Bridge over the River Kwai* (1957) and *Lawrence of Arabia* (1962), both of which won the Academy Award for best picture. When these films are included in lists of the best American films (such as the AFI's top 100 best films), their inclusion is justified usually on the basis of Americans being involved in some stage of production (producers, actors, etc.), but the true reason may well lie in the fact that one cannot list the greatest and most influential English-language films, films that Americans also have watched and loved, without including these films. Nevertheless, this paper will focus upon films made by American directors.

4 This issue was not addressed directly as such by early film theorists. Rather, in an effort to defend film as an art form in face of the argument that cinema would have primarily an affective influence both directly (through intentional use as propaganda) or indirectly, it appears that the reflective nature of film was emphasized over and against its affective nature from the early days of film theory until about 1968. See Anthony Easthope, "Classic Film Theory and Semiotics" in *The Oxford Guide to Film Studies*, 51–53, Ian Christie, "Formalism and Neo-Formalism" in *The Oxford Guide to Film Studies*, 58–59, and "Film and Reality" in *Film Theory and Criticism*, sixth edition, ed. Leo Braudy and Marshall Cohen (New York: Oxford University Press, 2004), 135–141.

5 Michael Medved in *Hollywood vs. America* (New York: HarperCollins Publishers, 1992) argues that the values of the Hollywood elite that are reflected in American cinema from about 1967 and on vie with the values of mainstream America and that this more than anything has led to a gradual decrease in movie-attendance from the late 1960s

and on. According to his argument, Americans long to see their values reflected on screen, but Hollywood reflects its own values, and so people have stopped going to the movies as much as they once did. See Medved, 3–4. (For arguments contra Medved see Andy Klein, "Weapons of Mass-Appeal Destruction," in *Los Angeles City Beat*, April 22, 2004, Laura M. Holson, "With Popcon, DVDs and TiVo, Moviegoers Are Staying Home," *The New York Times*, May 27, 2005, and "Movie Attendance Linked to Theatre Experience, Increased Competition for Consumer Time, According to PA Consulting Group Survey," *PR Newswire*, January, 4, 2007. In these articles it is argued that other factors are responsible for the decline in movie theatre attendance, including new technology, poorer quality of films (but not so much the values communicated in these films), and negative reactions to the cinema experience in and of itself despite the quality of any particular film.)
Thomas S. Hibbs in *Shows about Nothing: Nihilism in Popular Culture from* The Exorcist *to* Seinfeld (Dallas: Spence Publishing Company, 1999) argues that American cinema is shaping the worldview of mainstream America in ways that vie with our traditional democratic ideals. Where Medved argues that American film of the post-classical era of Hollywood film production (1967 on) reflects the values of the Hollywood elite, values at odds with mainstream America, Hibbs argues that American films (and television) of this same era have affected the American worldview, causing a shift in values where mainstream America more and more reflects the values of the Hollywood elite. See Hibbs, 3–9.

6 See Braudy and Cohen, "Preface" in *Film Theory and Criticism*, xv–xviii.

7 Easthope, 51–52.

8 Ibid, 51. It could be that in the early days of cinema, before film became a mainstay in American popular culture, people had to adjust to the fact that these images were not real. Nevertheless, some filmmakers still resort to gimmicks to get such an emotional, even physical, reaction from their audience. This is possible because the audience suspends its belief long enough to pretend that what is not real on the screen is real. Steven Spielberg has employed such techniques to similar effect in *Jaws* (1975) and other films.

9 Ibid, 51.

10 Ibid, 51–52.

11 Christie, 58–59.

12 Formalism was more technically a term used to describe especially Russian theories about filmmaking in the 1930s as theorists in the Soviet Union reacted to government efforts to use film strictly for propaganda. Creationism was a term used by theorists outside of Russia in the 1930s to defend film as an art form. The term "formalism" is now used commonly to refer generally to both of these theories. See Easthope, 52 and Christie, 58–59.

13 Easthope, 52 and Braudy and Cohen, *Film Theory and Criticism*, 137, 140.

14 Easthope, 53.

15 One realist who seemed to have emphasized both the reflective and affective nature of film was Siegfried Kracauer, a film theorist who studied German films of the inter-war period (1919–1939). He argued that films of this time period "revealed a fear of the emerging chaos and a disposition to submit to social authority." According to Kracauer, these films had the effect of fostering anti-democratic and passive attitudes and "strong sadism and an appetite for destruction" that are prominent "in the German collective soul." See Kracauer, "From *From Caligari to Hitler*: The Cabinet of Dr. Caligari," in *Film Theory and Criticism*, 162–164 and Douglas Kellner, "Hollywood Film and Society," in *The Oxford Guide to Film Studies*, 355.

16 Easthope, 52.

17 See Easthope, 52, and Braudy and Cohen, 135–141.

18 One might expect that the Realists would stress the effect of film, since the audience is to assume that what they are seeing is real—and this theory does seem to speak to the issue of how films are affective (see footnote 15 above). It appears, however, that

the substance of this debate was not so much how a film is affective but how a film is made and what it then counts as—a representation of real life (Realism) or a construct (Formalism).

[19] Easthope, 54–55.

[20] See Easthope, 52–56, Chuck Kleinhans, "Marxism and Film," in *The Oxford Guide to Film Studies*, 106ff, and Barbara Creed, "Film and Psychoanalysis" in *The Oxford Guide to Film*, 77ff. The label "Apparatus theory" is given to the Ideological approach especially to explain the psychological effect upon the viewer—the apparatus being the viewer, the screen, and the projector (Creed, 79–82).

[21] In my reading thus far, it does not appear as if any theorist associated with the Ideological approach is fully consistent with each element underlying this theory. This theory appears to be a label that covers various different approaches that make use of these theories.

[22] See especially Creed, 86-88.

[23] See Andrew Sarris, "Notes on the Auteur Theory in 1962" in *Film Theory and Criticism*, 561–564 and Peter Wollen, "The Auteur Theory" in *Film Theory and Criticism*, 565–567.

[24] Sarris, 561–563. It may appear that the task of determining who is and who is not an auteur could be quite subjective, leaving great room for personal opinion and preference. Nevertheless, there is a general consensus on who are the great directors of the past 100 plus years. One could, for instance, consult the AFI list of 100 Best Directors or other such lists.

[25] Two examples of "message films" would be *Reefer Madness* (1936) and *The China Syndrome* (1979). The former was a warning against the use of marijuana while the latter was a warning against nuclear power. The former is today something of a cult classic because of its value as "unintentional comedy" and camp; the latter was considered an important film at the time of its release but does not appear to be much watched today (i.e., I cannot find it at Blockbuster). The former was apparently ineffective in its attempt to influence American culture; the latter may have had some effect as American society does not depend heavily upon nuclear power.

[26] Wollen, 567–572.

[27] This pattern can be observed in two notable and critically-praised Hawks films, the western *Rio Bravo* (1959) and the comedy *Bringing Up Baby* (1938). The western depicts a male-dominated world where the male heroes are each men of action, highly skilled at what they do, and fully dependent upon one another as the action unfolds; the female lead must accept this reality to be accepted by these men, and she and the male lead come together only when the action of the film has been fully resolved. In the comedy a somewhat passive male lead is pursued by the aggressive female lead; throughout the story the male lead is put into humiliating situations against his will—e.g., forced to dress in a female nightgown at one point, later put in jail, and the like—and he ends up dependent upon the dominant female lead to resolve his troubles. Interestingly, the female characters in most Hawks films—both male-dominated action films and female-dominated comedies—have been considered some of the strongest female characters in the classical era of cinema, giving rise to the term "Hawksian woman archetype." Hawks' male characters, however, are only strong when found in the genre of drama or action.

[28] Wollen makes the connection between Hawks and structuralism, but does not develop it as I do here. See Wollen, 572.

[29] See Wollen, 572.

[30] See Robin Wood, "Ideology, Genre, Auteur" in *Film Theory and Criticism*, 717ff.

[31] The classical period of Hollywood film production (1929–1967) can be divided into two phases: The first phase (1929–1948) was the age of the studio system in which certain Hollywood-based companies owned both the means of the production of films and the theatres to which they were distributed. This was the age of studio-promoted stars and formulaic film plots. Although this era has been criticized for the restrictions the

studios placed upon filmmaking, some of the greatest directors made some of their greatest works in this time. This period came to an end as a result of the advent of television which now became the cinema's major competitor in the arena of popular entertainment and anti-trust laws that broke up the monopoly studios had on both production and distribution. The second phase of the classical period of Hollywood films (1949–1967) was characterized by efforts of Hollywood studios to compete with television amidst a steady decline in movie attendance. This decline eventually steadied out in the 1960s to a level of attendance which has been more or less static, at least through 2000 (see Michelle Pautz, "The Decline in Average Weekly Cinema Attendance: 1930–2000" in *Issues in Political Economy*, 2002, Vol. 11.) The post-classical period or the age of "New Hollywood" began in 1967 with the institution of the rating system and a crop of new directors whose films seemed to challenge the conventions and ideologies of Hollywood in the classical period. See "History of American Cinema" in *Encyclopedia Britannica*, CD edition, 2000.

32 See Wood, 717–718.

33 Ibid, 718.

34 Ibid, 718–719.

35 Point 7 may appear to clash openly with point 6. Wood explains that point 7 is a "convenient assumption" in a capitalist ideology: Those who do not have are nevertheless supposed to be happier than those who have—"the more oppressed you are, the happier you are." See Wood, 719.

36 Ibid, 719.

37 When reading through this list of values and archetypes, note that one does not necessarily need to use a Marxist paradigm, as does Wood, to detect these same values and archetypes in American films. I would argue that the average viewer, if asked, would be able to list some of these very same things.

38 Ibid, 719.

39 Or perhaps this is depicted in films of other genres—e.g., comedies—where the male lead, the character who should be the ideal male, now may become the clown and the butt of jokes.

40 Regarding this point, Paul A. Cantor argues in *Gilligan Unbound: Pop Culture in the Age of Globalization* (Lanham: Rowman and Littlefield Publishers, 2001) that the 1960s sitcom *Gilligan's Island*, what Cantor calls "the most successful bad show in the history of television," is a celebration of democratic ideals that is opposed to progress. Though the castaways don't realize it, their life is ideal as it is typified by the simpler, more rustic, pre-industrial way of life of the early American experience in which American democracy is rooted. See Cantor, 3–33.

41 This darkness in the actual lighting is explained in that these films were often produced with low budgets and thus did not always have adequate lighting. Thus there were literal economic reasons explaining why these films were so literally dark.

42 See Wood, 722 and Nicholas Christopher, *Somewhere in the Night: Film Noir and the American City* (New York: Free Press), 17.

43 While discussing *The Searchers* in a class on film at St. Paul's Lutheran Church in Des Peres, Missouri, I asked a question regarding the role of Edwards in rescuing Debbie. One member of the class answered succinctly and correctly, "Not to kill her."

44 See Hibbs, 25. Note that this film is top of the list in the AFI's list of 100 most inspirational films.

45 Wood, 721–723.

46 Ibid., 723.

47 Ibid., 722.

48 Hibbs, 24.

49 See Woods, 721 and Hibbs, 24–26.

50 These last two items are not included in Wood's list, but I add them here as I believe these too are values exemplified in American films of the classical age of Hollywood.

[51] Here I add the component of "mastery over others" to the traits listed by Wood. I do this for two reasons: we see this as an element in at least American auteur Howard Hawks' depiction of the ideal male (see again Wollen, 572). We also saw this in the John Ford/John Wayne depiction of Ethan Edwards in *The Searchers*. Here there could emerge another contradiction: for a society that holds up independence as an ideal, there is offered an archetype who embodies this ideal, and yet often in the story spends his time depriving others of their independence, autonomy, and, of course, very often their lives as well.

[52] I use the AV here because that English translation renders the imperative φρονεῖτε∘οφ φρονέω ("think," "have in mind")—with the word mind in the translation. Thus, given the influence of the AV rendering, this is perhaps one reason why Phil. 2:5 is matrixed as one of the "mind of Christ passages" among English-speaking churches; the NIV and NAS render the same concept as attitude (but one never hears of "the attitude of Christ"). I also prefer the way the AV renders the relative clause ὅ καὶ ἐν Χριστῷ᾿Ιησοῦ in a more literal and straightforward manner than does the RSV or ESV.

[53] Gerald F. Hawthorne also reads this section of parenesis (1:27--2:18) as a unit, calling it "Instructions to the Church" in his outline of the epistle. See Hawthorne, *Philippians* in *Word Bible Commentary* (Waco: Word Books, 1983), xlix.

[54] See also 1 Peter 5:5–6 and James 4:6–10 for passages that parallel Philippians 2—exhortations to humility and the promise of future exaltation.

[55] Although many editions, including Nestle-Aland and the Concordia Self-Study Bible (NIV), have Philippians 2:5 indented so to have it introduce a new paragraph, this is simply the convention of printing. I assert that the exhortation and hymn of Philippians 2:5–11 mirror the exhortations of 2:1–4 and that the Christological hymn is used to provide both the Gospel basis and the prime example for all that has preceded from the new thought that began in 2:1.

Media

Anthony A. Cook

Media as a Source of Information and Identity

The purpose of this essay is to explore media as a source of information and identity. Much of the contemporary research conducted in this area occurs within the social sciences and reflects the relativistic theories of post-positivism. While this essay incorporates observational insights from the social sciences, it does so as a handmaiden to faith—acknowledging a theological understanding of an objective reality frequently absent from many areas of postmodern studies. It is my hope to provide both an understanding of media as a source of information and identity and suggest uses of media within the Christian life.

What are Media?

Before we explore media as a source of information and identity, we must first answer the question, "What are media?" The word "media" has multiple definitions ranging from electronic communications to the various technology-dependent forms of information storage. For the purpose of this essay, "media" will be used synonymously with the term "mass communication" as defined by Charles R. Wright. Wright, known for his research in the area of the sociology of communication, offers the following working definition:

> ...it is directed toward relatively large, heterogeneous, and anonymous audiences; messages are transmitted publicly, often timed to reach most audience members simultaneously, and are transient in charter; the communicator tends to be,

or to operate within, a complex organization that may involve great expense.[1]

Wright's definition includes, but is not limited to, what is often considered to be the traditional forms of mass communication—television, radio, film, and various forms of mass-distributed print publications. Now that we have a working definition, it is necessary to understand the activities that media perform. For this, we turn to political scientist and communications theorist, Harold Lasswell.

Media Activities

Lasswell proposed three activities of mass communication: surveillance, correlation, and the transmission of social heritage from one generation to the next (socialization).[2] In 1959, Wright added a fourth activity, entertainment.[3] We will examine each individually.

Surveillance

While omniscience is out of human reach, media provide society with something of an all-seeing eye. Media survey the environment both locally and globally in order to deliver relevant and vital information from around the world directly to our living rooms, offices, and automobiles. Society has become so dependent on the function of surveillance, that when deprived of media exposure, we feel strangely disconnected from the global village that media-savvy Americans call "home."

The all-seeing eye of media, however, is not without its blind spots. Through both choice and necessity, media present an incomplete picture of global events. Media elevate to our attention the news and events that it finds important and/or advantageous to report. This "focusing of attention" by the media is referred to as "agenda-setting" and is best summarized by Bernard Cohen in his famous 1963 statement, "The press may not be successful much of the time in telling people what to think, but it is stunningly successful in telling its readers what to think about."[4] While it might be true that media are not successful in telling us what to think, media offer explanations of and editorials on reported events. This brings us to our second media activity: correlation.

Correlation

With the continuous flood of information that media provide, it is frequently helpful for the media to assist the consumer in interpreting and weighing the unprocessed information. Not all news stories are of equal importance nor are all news stories easily understood. The need to make sense of mass-distributed information has given birth to numerous commentators, editorialists, experts, and analysts. It is almost impossible to find a mass medium that does not provide correlation. From the meteorologist who interprets weather patterns to the war analyst who explains military strategy, media attempt to provide both information and meaning.

Even though correlation is helpful in making sense of the complex and ever-changing society in which we live, correlation can be misleading. Media interpretation can easily become media "spin" designed to benefit media partners and promote media viewpoints.[5] The fine line between the meaningful interpretation of facts and their intentional manipulation is easily crossed. It only takes a single viewing of a network's nightly news program to determine the political, social, and perhaps even ethical leanings of the network owners and advertisers. Through interpretation and commentary, media values are by necessity explicated. In many cases, careful attention to media correlation can deepen the viewers' understanding not only of the message, but also of the messenger.

Socialization

Socialization is one of the most controversial media activities. Lasswell described this activity as the transmission of social heritage from one generation to the next. In today's pluralistic society, the idea of a common social heritage desirable for generational transmission is somewhat foreign and to some, even offensive. Gerhard Casper in his presidential address to Stanford University's Class of 1997 addresses this issue:

> One's social heritage does not come neatly packaged in an ice cube that can be thawed for reference and use. Nor are we frozen into a particular culture. But it is not for the university in its institutional role to tell you to blend in or to remain separate, to embrace an "amalgam" or to reject it. Whether the United States is best understood as a "melting pot" or a "mosaic" you will decide ... If we at the university were not committed to interactive pluralism, education would become impossible.[6]

Casper places the responsibility of interpreting one's social heritage directly in the hands of the individual. The role of the institution, according to Casper, is to create an environment of interactive pluralism—allowing people of diverse social heritages to interact, while maintaining their diversity. Seen through pluralistic eyes, America's social heritage is that it has no single social heritage. America's tradition is that it accepts all traditions; America's value is that it values all values. The only traditions and values rejected in America are those that deny the validity of the traditions and values of others.

While promoting an environment of interactive pluralism within an institution such as a university is a noble idea, it is not the societal norm. Excluding those who intentionally choose to embrace a life of diversity, the average American lives a life of uni-cultural segregation. Linda Holtzman, in her book *Media Message,* addresses this very point.

> Through the process of socialization, we grow up learning the values of our culture. The vast majority of us grew up with little diversity, and the values and beliefs we were taught seemed real, central, and 'normal.' Often we experience no sense of a pluralist community that included different foods, religious practices, beliefs, or customs. Rather, these invisible norms instilled a sense that our way was the right or only way and that other ways were unusual, weird, abnormal, or wrong ... for many of us, the voids and gaps in our personal experience are filled exclusively by formal education and media.[7]

It is in the midst of society's struggle between the ideal of interactive pluralism and the practicality of uni-cultural segregation that media socialization takes place. The response of media to this struggle is generally two-pronged. The first prong is reflected in the emphasis of media on themes of social integration and cohesion. Elizabeth Perse, however, has observed that this approach can result in stereotyping and over-simplification of societal differences in favor of ratings, revenue, and the appeasement of the dominant social class:

> An emphasis on cohesion, however, can be dysfunctional. If mass communication ignores subgroups in society, regional and ethnic differences may be diminished, reducing cultural and intellectual diversity in society. Mass media content often is not a multifaceted presentation of societal norms and values. Unfortunately, because of demands of the marketplace, media content is often simplified, stereotyped, and representative of the dominant social class. Those images may lead to improper socialization and learning inaccurate, slanted representations of societal values.[8]

Comparing the insights of both Perse and Holtzman, we discover that media socialization exhibits the same dysfunctions attributed to socialization attempts in general. Both fail to provide socialization that truly embraces the actual diversity of American society. In the end, one wonders whether media promote actual societal values and cultural heritage or, through a combination of dysfunction and self-interest, fabricate a heritage that is diverse enough to appear inclusive, but narrow enough to retain the support of its heterogeneous viewers and sponsors. Robert Bellah, in his classic analysis of individualism and commitment in American life, put it this way:

> ...it would be difficult to argue that there is any coherent ideology or overall message that [television] communicates. There is a sense in which the broadcasters' defense of their role—that they are merely mirroring the culture—has a certain plausibility. They do not support any clear set of beliefs or policies, yet they cast doubt on everything ... While television does not preach, it nevertheless presents a picture of reality that influences us more than an overt message could.[9]

The difficulty of being all things to all people without offending anyone is the burden of the major media outlets and has resulted in the explosion of specialized media content. This approach, known as specialization, is the second prong of media's response to the difficulty of socialization.

Specialization is the process of creating media content aimed at a specific area of interest, ethnicity, or sub-section of society. This approach has begun to dominate media production and is evident in the panoply of specialized magazines, movies, and television stations. Many believe that specialization is the future of media content production as evidenced by the popularity of custom Internet news feeds, genre-specific satellite and Internet radio stations, downloadable television programs, and the increasing use of digital video recorders, all of which give the viewer greater control over media content and scheduling. While media specialists, such as British editor Nick Watson, see specialized media as "an information ghetto that stands only as one part among a collection of other such divided parts,"[10] others such as Bill Gates see specialization as the desired evolution of media production and delivery. In an interview on *The Daily Show with John Stewart*, Gates envisions the future impact of computer and Internet technology on the delivery of traditional media content:

> It [computer technology] is changing everything ... Even things like TV where you only have a certain number of channels and it's not very interactive. That can be revolutionized as we move it onto the Internet ... Say that you were watching the news—it would spend more time on the topics you were interested in and spend little or no time on things you don't care about.[11]

If Gates is correct, which I believe that he is, content specialization will not only change the future of media, but it will also have a profound impact on the activity of media socialization. In an age where the socialization of children is often done in the glow of a television screen and computer monitor, the potential effects of media socialization cannot be ignored.

Entertainment

Even though we might not intentionally turn to television for socialization, we eagerly turn to television for entertainment. While my colleague David Lewis skillfully addresses this fourth media activity in another essay, I would like to make one observation as it relates to media as a source of information and identity. Just as the jester of old used entertainment not only to amuse, but also to influence the perspective of the king, so too our modern jesters of media include subtle subtexts meant to do more than entertain. In, with, and under the laugh tracks and heart-touching stories, media creators weave their personal values and beliefs in the hopes of impacting viewer perspectives and swaying public opinion. So as we sit on our Lazy-Boy thrones seeking novel entertainment from our media jesters, we need to be aware of the media messages transmitted within our seemingly mindless entertainment.

Now that we have completed our prolegomena, we turn to the specific application of media as a source of information and identity.

Media as a Source of Information

In order to understand media as a source of information, it is helpful to first look at the process through which information is transmitted. In 1948, Claude E. Shannon[12] published a two-part article for the *Bell System Technical Journal* that included a groundbreaking model of a communications system.[13]

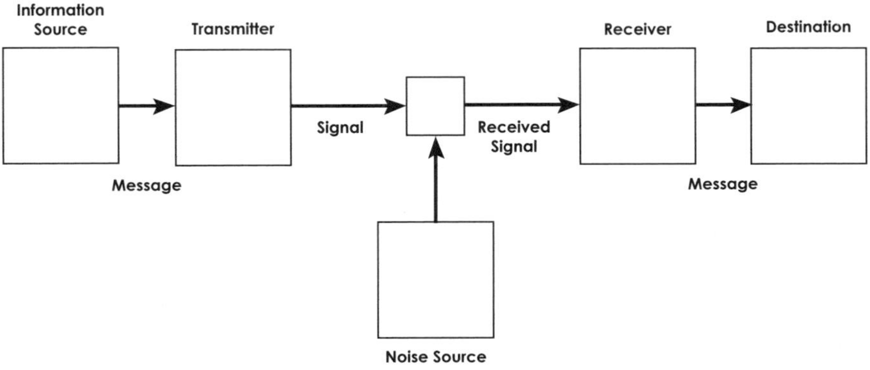

Shannon's communication model was popularized by another American scientist and mathematician named Warren Weaver. Shannon and Weaver co-authored a book containing a layman's version of Shannon's communication theory. The result of their work was the development of one of the most commonly used communication models, known as the Shannon-Weaver Model. The Shannon-Weaver Model is comprised of six elements: a source, an encoder, a message, a channel, a decoder, and a receiver. While Lasswell developed a similar model consisting of five core components, the Shannon-Weaver model has proven more effective in understanding technology-based communications such as those used in mass media. The transmitter encodes the message provided by the source into a signal that can be sent over a medium and then decoded by the receiver for presentation at the destination.

While the model produced by Shannon and Weaver presents the transmission of information in a clear and mechanical form, it does not explain the potential effects that the transmitted information has on the recipient. For this we must leave the world of mathematics and engineering and return to the world of sociology and psychology. The impact of information transmitted by the media has garnered considerable debate as society seeks to find a cause for the anti-social behavior so frequently reported on the nightly news. On one side of this growing debate, we find those who deny any connection between the information media transmits and the antisocial behavior of those who view it. On the other, we find those who believe that media has the ability to turn law-abiding citizens into cold-blooded killers by watching *The Basketball Diaries*, listening to *Helter Skelter* or by playing *Grand Theft Auto*. The truth, I believe, is found somewhere in between. While determining the strength of media effects is a difficult task, numerous studies show that heavy media viewers, such as children, are indeed impacted by media content. The following conclusions represent a sample of the findings regarding media effects:[14]

> By the time a child is eighteen years old, he or she will witness on television (with average viewing time) 200,000 acts of violence including 40,000 murders (Huston, et al, 1992).
>
> Children, ages 8 to 18, spend more time (44.5 hours per week-6 ½ hours daily) in front of computer, television, and game screens than any other activity in their lives except sleeping (Kaiser Family Foundation, 2005).
>
> Since the 1950s, more than 1,000 studies have been done on the effects of violence in television and movies. The majority of these studies conclude that: children who watch significant

amounts of television and movie violence are more likely to exhibit aggressive behavior, attitudes and values (Senate Committee on the Judiciary, 1999).

Media violence affects children's behavior states the American Medical Association, American Academy of Pediatrics, American Psychological Association, American Academy of Family Physicians, and American Academy of Child & Adolescent Psychiatry (Congressional Public Health Summit, 2000).

Children are affected at any age, but young children are most vulnerable to the effects of media violence (Bushman, 2001). Young children are more easily impressionable, have a harder time distinguishing between fantasy and reality, cannot easily discern motives for violence, learn by observing and imitating.

Young children who see media violence have a greater chance of exhibiting violent and aggressive behavior later in life, than children who have not seen violent media (Congressional Public Health Summit, 2000).

Violent video games can cause people to have more aggressive thoughts, feelings, and behaviors; and decrease empathetic, helpful behaviors with peers (Anderson, 2004; Gentile, 2003).

Children who watch more TV and play more video games are not only exposed to more media violence, but are more likely to act more aggressively with peers and tend to assume the worst in their interactions with peers (Buchanan, et al, 2002).

Violence (homicide, suicide, and trauma) is a leading cause of death for children, adolescents and young adults, more prevalent than disease, cancer or congenital disorders (American Academy of Pediatrics, 2001).

Such findings can lead to various interpretations. But it is my opinion that the debate concerning the existence of media effects can be easily answered through simple observation. The fact that we laugh at sitcoms, are frightened by horror films, are calmed by soothing music, are agitated by the editorial column in the daily news, and demonstrate increased aggression while watching televised sports, proves that the unknown producers of mass media can impact us emotionally, psychologically, and even behaviorally. Over the years, four different models have been developed to explain the nature of media effects and the variables involved.

TABLE 1

Comparing the Four Models of Media Effects[15]

	Nature of Effects	Media Content Variables	Audience Variables
Direct	Immediate, uniform, observable Short-term Emphasis on change Cognitive and affective; behavioral effects possible	Salience, arousal, and realism	Not relevant
Conditional	Individualized Reinforcement as well as change Cognitive, affective, and behavioral effects possible Long- or short-term	Not relevant	Social categories Social relationships Individual differences
Cumulative	Based on cumulative exposure Cognitive or affective effects Rarely behavioral Enduring Effects	Constant across channels Repetition	Not relevant
Cognitive-transactional	Immediate and short-term Based on one-shot exposure Cognitive and affective; behavioral effects possible	Salience of visual cues	Schema make-up Mood Goals

While I believe that each of the above-mentioned models contains a piece of the media effects puzzle, it is my assertion that no one model presents the complete picture. While lacking appropriate credentials in sociology and psychology, I will nonetheless propose my own hybrid solution.

TABLE 2

A Proposed Model of Media Effects

Nature of Effects	Media Content Variables	Audience Variables
Immediate, delayed, and cumulative effects possible Individualized Cognitive, affective, and behavioral effects possible Long- or short term	Saliency, arousal, realism, content, structure, and framing	Social context, worldview, knowledge, individual differences, mood, and schema activation

Nature of Media Effects

I would contend that media, for all intents and purposes, should be treated as a drug. Taking a moment to extend the metaphor, one begins to ask provocative questions concerning media dosage, age appropriateness, tolerance, proper usage, addiction, and potential side effects. Let's take a moment to explore media's drug-like effects.

As with drugs, the effects of media consumption can be immediate, delayed and/or cumulative. Immediate effects include potential cognitive dissonance, changes in mood, and physical responses such as salivation and arousal. While many media effects fall into this category, some effects take longer to "work through" the viewer's system and/or are activated only when combined with other stimuli. Take for example a child, who after watching a report of a local burglary, experiences fright hours later while attempting to sleep, or a co-worker who begins to spontaneously laugh after finally processing the meaning of a punch line heard in a movie the previous night. The temporal separation of the media event from the media effect creates not only a "flashback," but demonstrates the ability of media to transfer its power outside of its original context—impacting the viewer in potentially negative and unexpected ways.

The third type of media effect, the cumulative effect, is difficult to predict and potentially devastating for both the individual and society. Similar to the "dulling of the eyes" of the frequent marijuana user or the liver failure of a lifelong alcoholic, cumulative media effects can occur in habitual users and have long-term effects. Suspected cumulative media effects include: desensitization to violence, increase in anti-social behavior, reduction of attention span, and neurological changes in the information-processing pathways of the brain. The line between the short-term effects of occasional media use and the long-term cumulative effects of heavier users is different for every person and should be frequently monitored.

Media Content Variables

Like drugs, for media content to have the intended effect, media producers must blend the necessary ingredients in the correct proportions. Media producers invest considerable time and money attempting to understand the chemistry of media creation. One of the most important ingredients is media saliency. Does the media content have the necessary qualities needed to capture the attention of the viewers as they are clicking through the television channels, scanning the radio dial, or flipping through the pages of a newspaper or magazine? In a society where people spend most of their time multitasking, media producers need to be able to draw viewer attention away from competing sources in order to produce the maximum media effect.

Once the viewer's attention has been captured, the artful task of delivering the desired information while retaining viewer attention begins. In the case of television, the use of different camera angles, frequent visual changes, musical scores, and appealing images help to produce the sensory stimulation necessary to "gain a hearing" for the transmitted information. Other factors such as the realism of the images portrayed, the themes and scenarios used to frame the information, and the quality and perceived relevancy of the content are all ingredients that can give media the desired potency.

Audience Variables

Formulation alone, however, does not guarantee that the desired media effect will be achieved nor does it assure that negative side effects will not occur. Just as the same drug can produce differing effects in different people, not all media viewers are affected by media information in the same way. The differences in viewer "chemistry" mediate effects even during simultaneous exposure. Social context, worldview, knowledge, age, gender, ethnicity, mood, and past experiences all impact how media information is received and the resulting effects.

As we conclude our look at media as a source of information, we must remember the potential dangers. Media information is influenced and shaped by hidden agendas, biased interpretations, and the desire for financial gain. It is the responsibility of the media consumers to carefully choose both the type of media they are exposed to and the frequency at which they are exposed. Media should be treated as any other potentially dangerous substance that we allow into our homes, bodies, and lives.

In our pursuit for information, we need to seek the most reliable source, view it critically, and constantly subject our findings to the authority of God's Word. As people of faith, we rely on God's Word and the gift of sanctified reason to guide us through the endless jungle of media content. As parents, it is our responsibility to protect our children from negative media effects. In the same way that parents would not administer a drug to their child without first understanding what it contained and its potential side effects, parents should not allow their children access to media without first examining its content and weighing the potential costs. Parents should be encouraged to use their remotes and computer keyboards to limit access to inappropriate media and to teach moderation. Media selection and moderation are the keys to responsible media consumption.

Parents should also be encouraged to consider their child's unique emotional, psychological, and spiritual "chemistry" when selecting media. Just because a child meets the minimum age requirements for a particular video game or film, does not mean that the child is ready to cope with the specific media content or that the media effects are guaranteed to be beneficial. In the end, regardless of the viewer's age, media needs to be used with discretion and in a way that is consistent with our Christian calling.

Media as a Source of Identity

When Adam and Eve fell into sin, their sociological, biological, psychological, and theological identities changed. Misinformed by a persuasive serpent and tempted by an alternate view of reality and truth, they turned their backs on God. As a result, Adam and Eve, along with the subsequent human race, were thrown into an identity crisis of Biblical proportions. As they stood outside the garden gates, one can imagine that they asked themselves the now all-too-familiar Eriksonian question, "Who am I?"[16]

From that point on, the fallen human race has attempted to define itself apart from God and if recent studies are correct, media and Internet technologies might bring us one step closer to achieving this goal. Sherry Turkle, a sociology professor at MIT and clinical psychologist, made the following observations about the role of technology in identity creation:

> In the story of constructing identity in the culture of simulation, experiences on the Internet figure prominently, but these experiences can only be understood as part of a larger cultural context. That context is the story of eroding boundaries between the real and the virtual, the animate and the inanimate, the unitary and the multiple self, which is occurring both in advanced scientific fields or research and the patterns of everyday life. From scientists trying to create artificial life to children "morphing" through a series of virtual personae, we shall see evidence of fundamental shifts in the way we create and experience human identity.[17]

The Internet, classified by some as a medium and by others as a message, holds the potential to revolutionize not only the field of communication studies, but also our understanding of personal identity. Take, for example, the author of this essay. At any one time I maintain at least two distinct, yet concurrent, virtual identities. In one computer window I am Tony and in the other I am Culinarius, the 25th-level Warlock in the Internet-based massive multiplayer game *The World of Warcraft*. Now you are probably thinking to yourself, "Alright, but in reality Tony only has one identity and the others are just make-believe." This might be true for anyone over thirty, but for those who have been raised with the Internet, the definition of "reality" has more to do with personal perception and relationships than it does objective truth. In fact, the claim that this is a reality that exists outside the individual is one of the great postmodern blasphemies. While modern thinkers might equate this understanding of identity as little more than changing masks or "wearing multiple hats," postmodern thinkers have the ability to embrace multiple identities at once. Turkle describes this new view of identity as "the sum total of your distributed presence." So where does this new and somewhat sci-fi notion of identity lead? It leads to what I like to call the Patchwork Persona.

The Patchwork Persona

The theory of a Patchwork Persona equates the modern concept of self-identity to a patchwork quilt. Each patch represents an individual aspect of human life and the way in which the individual interprets it. When a "hole" in the fabric of interpretation is found, the individual attempts to find a patch that effectively makes sense of that particular aspect of human life. Patches can be collected from different religious, traditional, philosophical, and political ideals. The only prerequisite is that the patch effectively fills the hole of interpretation with a meaning that is acceptable to the individual. Over a period of time, patches can be replaced with other patches found by the individual to be more effective in providing meaning for that particular aspect of human life. Some patches are outgrown, while others are purposely removed as vestiges of indoctrination or social baggage. These seemingly contradictory patches are held together by the belief that our self-made fabric of interpretation doesn't need to be consistent in ideology or source, but merely effective in creating meaning.

When a hole is found or created through the removal of an "ineffective" patch, the individual becomes open to suggestions from various sources including media. No longer are ideas and beliefs rejected or accepted because they are "Christian" or "Lutheran" or "Midwestern." These titles are perceived to be external labels from another time and cannot be considered to have a defining effect on an individual's perception of the world or personal reality. Combine this with the growing choices of easily accessible specialized media and the individual has all the resources needed to create a completely customized Patchwork Persona. It appears that John Dewey was onto something when he said, "The self is not something ready-made, but something in continuous formation through choice of action."[18]

As much as I like my theory, I have to admit that it is inherently flawed and that it illustrates mankind's loss of its true identity instead of its gain. Like most postmodern philosophies, it places the individual at the center of reality—the power and right that only the Creator possesses is attributed to the individual. But returning to our story of Adam and Eve, we discover that this has been our problem all along. Adam and Eve sought another medium that conveyed a message pleasing to their sense, but instead of finding identity ("You will be like God"), they lost the identity they had been given by God. Any attempt to find who we are and who we are becoming outside of God is futile. Even Nietzsche knew that obtaining a clear understanding of reality from the human perspective is impossible when he said, "We know no fact independent of interpretation; there is no vision of reality untainted by prejudice and perspective."[19] So instead of seeking other medium that are tainted by prejudice and perspective, wouldn't it be easy and ultimately more effective to return to the one medium through which information is given without spin and identity, revealed without tainted interpretation? For in the end, even though Adam and Eve's original identity was destroyed through sin, through the work of Jesus Christ our true identity is restored.

As Christians, we have the wonderful opportunity of providing the patch-seeking people of this world with a comprehensive and unified fabric—the robe of Christ's righteousness—through which true meaning, identity, and life is found. But before this can happen, we must ensure that our identity and the identities of our children are found in Christ, lest we fall prey to the deceptive agendas and misinformation of this multi-media world.

At the dawn of the last century, innovative Lutheran American minds took hold of a new wave of emerging media and technologies to broadcast (literally) an exciting Gospel message to a national, and eventually a worldwide, audience. First in radio, then in television, Lutheran pastors and laypeople took the lead in utilizing these media as a space where the American mind would meet the mind of Christ.

At the dawn of this new century, new media and new technologies are emerging virtually every day. The Internet was only the beginning. Just like in the last century, these media pose a challenge to our individual and collective sense of identity and to the ways we access information and obtain knowledge. Where previously our culture could assume continuity and coherence—whole communities of people gathering before their radio or television on the same day, at the same time, to listen to their favorite programs—now our computers, DVRs, and smart phones make our lives more fragmented, more decentered, more patch-worked.

But in the challenge is the opportunity. The Gospel word of hope speaks the same power to make wounded hearts whole. The robe of Christ's righteousness still clothes God's children with meaning and identity. There is great opportunity in this new world of media and technology, and the world awaits those who are ready to take hold of it. Many people already are, but there is still vast potential. Is there a new group of innovative Lutheran American minds ready to shape this new media with a Gospel message for a new century? How do these new media change the shape of that message? Is there an "interactive plurality" of Lutheran pastors and laypeople ready to see opportunity in the midst of challenge? The church is just such an interactive plurality in the best sense of the word.

All that awaits us is a new meeting of the minds.

Endnotes

1 Charles R. Wright, *Mass Communication: A Sociological Perspective*, 2nd ed. (New York: Random House, 1975), 8.
2 Harold D. Lasswell, "The Structure of Communication in Society" in *The Communications of Ideas*, ed. L. Bryson (New York: Harper & Brothers, 1948).
3 Charles R. Wright, *Mass Communication: A Sociological Perspective*, 2nd ed. (New York: Random House, 1975), 9.
4 Bernard C. Cohen, *The Press and Foreign Policy* (Princeton, NJ: Princeton University Press, 1963).
5 The word "spin" meaning to "tell a tale" can be found in James Hardy Vaux's 1812 book, *A New and Comprehensive Vocabulary of the Flash Language*. Flash was the slang vocabulary of the London underworld and Australian convicts. In America, the word "spin" was first applied to the CIA in the late 1970s and the media in the 1980s. The term came into the popular parlance during the 1990 presidential election.
6 Gerhard Casper, "Concerning Culture and Cultures," Welcome Address to the Class of 1997 and Their Parents, 23 September, 1993; available from http://www.stanford.edu/dept/pres-provost/president/speeches/930923culture.html; accessed 2 February, 2007.
7 Linda Holtzman, *Media Message: What Film, Television, And Popular Music Teach us About Race, Class, Gender, And Sexual Orientation* (Armonk, NY: M.E. Sharpe, 2000). 11–12.
8 Elizabeth M. Perse, *Media Effects and Society* (Mahwah, NJ: Lawrence Erlbaum Associates, Inc., 2001), 56.
9 Robert N. Bellah, Richard Madsen, William M. Sullivan, Ann Swidler, and Steven M. Tipton, *Habits of the Heart: Individualism and Commitment in American Life* (New York: Harper and Row, 1986; originally published, Berkeley: University of California Press, 1985), 279.
10 Nick Watson, "A Deeply Dilettante Review," *The Argotist*, February, 1996.
11 This excerpt is taken from "The Daily Show with John Stewart"; viewed 29 January, 2007.
12 Not only is Claude Shannon the father of information theory, his 1937 master's thesis pioneered the use of Boolean algebra as a way to mathematically simplify the electronic components used in digital circuit design.
13 Claude E. Shannon, "A Mathematical Theory of Communication," *Bell System Technical Journal*, vol. 27, pp. 379–423, 623–656, July, October, 1948.

[14] National Institute on Media and the Family, "Children and Media Violence Fact Sheet"; available from http://www.mediafamily.org/facts/facts_vlent.shtml; accessed 3 February, 2007.
[15] Adapted from Elizabeth M, Perse, *Media Effects and Society*, 51.
[16] Erik Erikson (1902–1994) was a German-born psychologist famous for expanding Sigmund Freud's theory of stages to an eight-stage theory of personality development. He is also credited with coining of the term "identity crisis."
[17] Sherry Turkle, *Life on the Screen: Identity in the Age of the Internet* (New York: Touchstone, 1997), 14.
[18] John Dewey, Democracy and Education: Complete and Unabridged (Seven Treasures Publications, 2008), 225.
[19] Cited in Bruce Lawrence, *Defenders of God: The Fundamentalist Revolt against the Modern Age* (San Francisco: Harper & Row, 1989), 90.

SOLI DEO GLORIA

Contributors

Joel Biermann teaches systematic theology at Concordia Seminary, St. Louis. He is married to Jeannalee and has three children: Jasmine, Justine, and Jess.

Anthony A. Cook teaches practical theology at Concordia Seminary, St. Louis, in the areas of education and postmodern studies. He also serves as director of distance curricula and editor of Concordia Seminary's iTunes University. His current area of research is the European emerging church movement. He is married to Elizabeth and they have a son, Ben.

Robert Kolb is mission professor emeritus of systematic theology and former director of the Institute for Mission Studies at Concordia Seminary, St. Louis. He has published widely in Reformation studies. His most recent volume, *Martin Luther: Confessor of the Faith*, was published in 2009 by Oxford University Press. He and his wife Pauline reside in St. Louis, Missouri.

R. Reed Lessing teaches exegetical theology (Old Testament) and is director of the graduate school at Concordia Seminary, St. Louis. He is author of the *Amos* and *Jonah* commentaries in the Concordia Commentary Series and is currently at work on *Isaiah* 40-55 (2011) and *Isaiah* 56-66. He is married to Lisa and has three children: Abi, Jonathan, and Lori.

David I. Lewis teaches exegetical theology (New Testament) at Concordia Seminary, St. Louis, where he also pursues teaching and research in film studies. He is married to Karen. They have three children: John, Marissa, and Courtney.

Dale A. Meyer currently serves as the tenth president of Concordia Seminary, St. Louis, where he teaches practical theology. He served in the Gregg H. Benidt Memorial Endowed Chair in Homiletics and Literature at Concordia from 2001-2005. He is the host of "The Meyer Minute," a weekday Internet and radio commentary. From 1989 to 2001 Dr. Meyer was speaker on the radio program "The Lutheran Hour" and until 2003 he was the host of the television show "On Main Street." He is married to Diane. They have two grown daughters, Elizabeth and Catharine.

Joel P. Okamoto teaches systematic theology at Concordia Seminary, St. Louis. He is married to Ruth, and has three children: Jacob, Peter, and Thomas.

Paul W. Robinson chairs the department of historical theology at Concordia Seminary, St. Louis. His most recent book is *Martin Luther: A Life Reformed*, published by Pearson in 2009. He and his wife Jane have three children: Emily, William, and James.

Leopoldo A. Sánchez M. teaches systematic theology in the Werner R. H. Krause and Elizabeth Ringger Krause Endowed Chair for Hispanic Ministries and is the director of the Center for Hispanic Studies at Concordia Seminary, St. Louis. He is currently working on *Oración y Vocación*, his second book for Editorial Concordia's *Biblioteca Teológica Concordia* series. He is married to Tracy. They have two children, Lucas and Ana.

David R. Schmitt teaches practical theology in the Gregg H. Benidt Memorial Endowed Chair in Homiletics and Literature at Concordia Seminary, St. Louis. His recent work explores how art, faith, and aesthetic sensibility can be joined together in the preaching task. Before this, he focused on rhetorical structures in homiletics, the integration of literary theory and preaching, and the art of pastoral discernment in preaching.